Philebus

PLATO

Philebus

Translated,
with Introduction
& Notes, by

DOROTHEA FREDE

HACKETT PUBLISHING COMPANY
Indianapolis/Cambridge

Plato: ca. 428–347 B.C.

Printed in the United States of America

02 01 00 99 98   2 3 4 5 6 7 8 9

For further information, please address the publisher:

Hackett Publishing Company, Inc.
P.O. Box 44937
Indianapolis, Indiana 46244-0937

Cover design by Listenberger Design & Associates

Interior design by Dan Kirklin

Library of Congress Cataloging-in-Publication Data

Plato.
    [Philebus. English]
    Philebus / Plato ; translated, with introduction & notes, by
Dorothea Frede.
       p.   cm.
    Includes bibliographical references.
    ISBN 0-87220-171-6 (cloth: alk. paper).
    ISBN 0-87220-170-8 (pbk.: alk. paper).
    1. Pleasure. I. Frede, Dorothea, 1941–   . II. Title.
B381.A5F7 1993
171'.4—dc20   93-587
                                                  CIP

Contents

Preface

Plato's dialogues need no recommendation. Presenting one of the less well known dialogues like the *Philebus* in a new translation, however, offers an occasion to explain its importance and the problems that make this work difficult to approach.

The importance of the *Philebus* is twofold. First of all, its main problem, the role of pleasure and knowledge as determining factors of human life, exercised Plato throughout his life. It is therefore of considerable interest how it is finally settled in the *Philebus*, a dialogue he wrote late in his life. Second, the search for the human good is here not embedded in the larger vista of an ideal community, as it is in the *Republic* and in the *Laws*. Plato rather approaches the topic from a metaphysical angle to determine the nature of pleasure and knowledge themselves, bringing to bear the full set of his dialectical tools to give the problems the comprehensive treatment they deserve. This dialectical approach to settle the question of the ultimate aim in our lives seems to take up a promise of long standing, the promise of a longer, fuller way of treating the manifold problem of virtue and the good that Socrates envisaged in the *Republic* (435d; 504b). The longer way taken in the *Philebus* does not provide us with all the information that is missing in the *Republic*, for Plato has not given up his reserved way of treating philosophical problems. In fact he seems to have made Socrates the main speaker once again, precisely because no "final" treatment is intended, but a discursive examination with suggestions and innuendoes that may go far, but never quite far enough to settle the questions in such a way that the reader could claim full comprehension of a definite doctrine. In short, Plato remains Plato, the philosopher who refuses to fix his reader's mind about his ultimate intentions. If the *Philebus* thus does not present us with Plato's final words on the Good that would settle all problems, this dialogue nevertheless contains a wealth of information, since it takes up problems in all areas that have been addressed by Plato earlier, viz. the theory of Forms, the method of dialectic, its presuppositions and application, and important questions of psychology as they relate to the question of the Good itself, of what makes a human life good and worthwhile. All these issues turn out to be inextricably intertwined, and that is precisely the reason why this new treatment of the competition between pleasure and knowledge at first presents formidable obstacles to the reader's comprehension. The dialogue's concluding words that there is "still a little missing," while they amount to a great understatement, still sum up at the same time the challenge for the reader to see how much is actually solved and what is still missing in the search for the Good.

Because of the obstacles to the reader's comprehension, the translation is accompanied not only by notes appended to the text, but also by a lengthy introductory essay with an analysis of the dialogue. This analysis is not meant as a substitute for the text, but rather as a short running commentary that is best read as a companion to it. Its divisions therefore follow the headings in the table of contents, which are also used to divide up the text. Nor is the analysis meant to supply what Plato himself refuses to deliver, the last word on the topic. Given Plato's open-ended way of dealing with his problems, the interpreter can do no more than provide a very tentative guide through the text. The essay and notes do not pretend to give an adequate scholarly treatment of the main philosophical issues. It is not possible within the framework of this volume to give an overview of the various approaches in the extensive secondary literature. The bibliography contains a representative selection of the literature, which the student of the *Philebus* may want to consult.

Rendering a difficult Platonic dialogue into English for the "Greekless reader" is always a challenge, since a translation must aspire to clarity and readability, while doing justice to the character of the original. If this is a hard enough task under any circumstances, it presented daunting difficulties for this nonnative speaker of English; it turned out to be a fascinating but also a humbling experience. A more than heavy burden has therefore fallen on Marjorie Grene, who corrected the various versions of my English translation as well as the introduction and the notes. Her generous advice was not limited to linguistic problems, but extended also to problems of interpretation. Words of gratitude seem therefore a rather poor compensation for the work she did to make up for the deficiencies of my work. She has acted as my unfailing consultant and confidant during all my twenty years of academic life in the United States. My gratitude also extends to the anonymous reader of the manuscript for many valuable suggestions and penetrating critical questions, which have prevented mistakes great and small, both in linguistic and in philosophical matters.

Dorothea Frede
Hamburg
January 1, 1993

Selected Bibliography

Allan, M.J.B. *Marsilio Ficino. The Philebus-Commentary: A Critical Edition and Translation.* Los Angeles: 1975.

Badham, C. *The Philebus of Plato.* London 1878².

Bringmann, K. "Platons Philebos und Herakleides Pontikos' Dialog *peri hedones.*" *Hermes* 100 (1972), 523–530.

Burkert, W. *Lore and Science in Ancient Pythagoreanism.* (trans.) Cambridge, Mass.: 1972.

Bury, R. G. *The Philebus of Plato.* Cambridge: 1897.

Cherniss, H. *Aristotle's Criticism of Plato and the Academy.* Baltimore: 1944.

———. *The Riddle of the Early Academy.* Berkeley and Los Angeles: 1945.

Cooper, N. "Pleasure and Goodness in Plato's *Philebus. Philosophical Quarterly* 18 (1968), 12–15.

Crombie, I. M. *An Examination of Plato's Doctrines.* vol. 2, London: 1963.

Dancy, R. M. "The One, the Many, and the Forms." *Ancient Philosophy* 4 (1984), 160–193.

Davidson, D. *Plato's Philebus.* New York: 1990 (Harvard Dissertation Reprint, submitted 1949).

de Vogel, C. J. "La théorie de l'*apeiron* chez Platon et dans la tradition plato-nicienne," *Philosophia Part 1 Studies in Greek Philosophy*, Assen: 1970, 378–395.

Diès, A., Platon, *Philèbe, Oeuvres Complets.* vol. 9, Paris: 1959².

Dybikowski, J. C. "False Pleasure and the *Philebus.*" *Phronesis* 25 (1970), 147–165.

Fahrnkopf, R. "Forms in the *Philebus.*" *Journal of the History of Philosophy* 15 (1977), 202–207.

Findlay, J. N. *Plato: The Written and Unwritten Doctrines.* London: 1974.

Fine, G. "Knowledge and *logos* in the *Theaetetus.*" *Philosophical Review* 88 (1979), 366–397.

Fowler, H. N. *Philebus.* London: 1925 (The Loeb Classical Library).

Frede, D. "Rumpelstiltskin's Pleasures: True and False Pleasures in Plato's *Philebus.*" *Phronesis* 30 (1985), 151–180.

———. "The Soul's Silent Dialogue—a Non-Aporetic Reading of the Theaetetus." *Proceedings of the Cambridge Philological Society* 215 (1989), 20–49.

———. "Disintegration and Restoration: Pleasure and Pain in Plato's Philebus." (ed.) R. Kraut, *The Cambridge Companion to Plato.* Cambridge: 1992, 425–463.

Gadamer, H. G. *Plato's Dialectical Ethics* (trans. R. M. Wallace). New Haven: 1991.

Gaiser, K. "Plato's Enigmatic Lecture 'On the Good'." *Phronesis* 25 (1980), 5–37.

Gallop, D. "Plato and the Alphabet." *Philosophical Review* 72 (1963), 364–376.

Gosling, G.C.B. "False Pleasures: *Philebus* 35c–41b." *Phronesis* 4 (1959), 44–54.
——. Father Kenny n False Pleasures in Plato's *Philebus*. *Phronesis* 5 (1960), 41–5.
——. *Plato: Philebus, Translated with Notes and Commentary*. Oxford: 1975.
—— and C. C. W. Taylor. *The Greeks on Pleasure*. Oxford: 1984.
Hackforth, R. *Plato's Examination of Pleasure, A Translation of the Philebus, with Introduction and Commentary*. Cambridge: 1954.
Hahn, R. "On Plato's *Philebus* 15b1–8," *Phronesis* 23 (1978), 158–172.
Hampton, C. "Pleasure, Truth and Being in Plato's *Philebus*: A Reply to Professor Frede," *Phronesis* 32 (1987), 252–262.
——. *Pleasure, Knowledge, and Being: An Analysis of Plato's Philebus*. Albany: 1990.
Jackson, H. "Plato's Later Theory of Ideas." *Journal of Philology* 10 (1882), 253–298.
Kenny, A. "False Pleasures in the *Philebus*: A Reply to Mr. Gosling." *Phronesis* 5 (1960), 45–52.
Kolb, D. "Pythagoras Bound: Limit and Unlimited in Plato's *Philebus*." *Journal of the History of Philosophy* 21 (1983), 497–511.
Letwin, O. "Interpreting the *Philebus*." *Phronesis* 26 (1981), 187–206.
Mohr, R., "*Philebus* 55c–62a and Revisionism." in (edd.) F. J. Pelletier and J. King-Farlow, *New Essays on Plato*. Guelph, Ont.: 1983, 165–170.
Moravcsik, J. "Forms, Nature, and the Good in the *Philebus*." *Phronesis* 24 (1979), 81–101.
Penner, T. M. "False Anticipatory Pleasures: *Philebus* 36a3–41a6." *Phronesis* 15 (1970), 166–178.
Richter, L. *Zur Wissenschaftslehre von der Musik bei Platon und Aristoteles*. Berlin: 1961.
Ryle, G. "Letters and Syllables in Plato." *Philosophical Review*, 69 (1960), 431–451.
Sayre, K. *Plato's Late Ontology: A Riddle Resolved*. Princeton: 1983.
——. "The *Philebus* and the Good." *Proceedings of the Boston Area Colloquium in Ancient Philosophy* 2 (1987), 45–71.
Schofield, M. "Who were *hoi duschereis* in Plato, *Philebus* 44a ff.?" *Museum Helveticum* 28 (1971), 2–20.
Shiner, R. *Knowledge and Reality in Plato's Philebus*. Assen: 1974.
——. "Must *Philebus* 59a–c Refer to Transcendent Forms?" *Journal of the History of Philosophy* 17 (1979), 71–77.
——. "Knowledge in the *Philebus* 55c–62a: A Response." in (edd.) F. J. Pelletier and J. King-Farlow, Guelph, Ont.: 1983, 171–183.
Stenzel, J. *Plato's Method of Dialectic*. trans. D. J. Allan, Oxford: 1940.
Striker, G. *Peras und Apeiron*. Göttingen: 1970.
Taylor, A. E. *Philebus and Epinomis*. London: 1956.
Trevaskis, J. R. "Classification in the *Philebus*." *Phonesis* 5 (1960), 39–44.

————. "Division and Its Relation to Dialectic and Ontology in Plato." *Phronesis* 12 (1967), 118–129.

von Fritz, K. "The Philosophical Passage in the Seventh Platonic Letter and the Problem of Plato's 'Esoteric' Philosophy." *Essays in Ancient Greek Philosophy*. (edd.) J. P. Anton and G. L. Kustas, Albany: 1971, 408–447.

Waterfield, R.A.H. "The Place of the *Philebus* in Plato's Dialogues." *Phronesis* 25 (1980), 270–303.

————. *Plato Philebus*. (Translation with Introduction), Harmondsworth: 1982.

Westerink, L. G. (ed. and trans.) *Damascius, Lectures on the Philebus, Wrongly Attributed to Olympiodorus*. Amsterdam: 1959.

Introductory Essay

1. The general character of the dialogue and its purpose.

The *Philebus* is a Platonic dialogue that is not commonly found on the undergraduate's reading list. If it is studied at all, it is reserved for the arcane discussions of graduate seminars or for specialists in late Platonic philosophy. Given the dialogue's topic and form, however, it is at first rather surprising that it should lead such a shadow existence. For here we have, once again, a discussion conducted by Socrates and a typically Socratic topic, the rivalry between pleasure and knowledge as the supreme good in human life. Not only that, the discussion is lively and recalls the old exchanges in the early Platonic dialogues between Socrates and some of his true-to-life partners. The partner is here not reduced to monotonous ayes and nays, as he is in so many other later dialogues.

But the impression that we are back with the old Socrates here and that there is a Socratic agenda does not last long, for once the lively altercations of the introductory scene are over, readers will find themselves immersed in discussions that seem remote in content and style from the Socratic questioning of old.[1] The development of the conversation seems quite un-Socratic, in that we have to spend considerable time in a kind of purgatory (or hell, as some might say) of methodological ruminations that are typical for some of the late Platonic works, before we even reach the promised field of investigation of the dialogue's avowed topic, pleasure and knowledge themselves. Getting through that purgatory is not an easy task, for it seems to presuppose a proper understanding of Platonic dialectic as it is deployed elsewhere. Novices who have not tried to penetrate the difficulties of the *Parmenides* or the *Sophist*, or have found them impenetrable, will find the *Philebus'* purgatory unappealing. And they will not be encouraged by the fact that the experts are far from agreed on the content and purpose of the dialectico-metaphysical first part, for there seem to be as many different interpretations as there are contributions.

Once that purgatory is over, neither is the long critical discussion of different kinds of pleasure and knowledge any green meadow in a philosopher's paradise. The dialogue's third part seems rather to be a barren field of unusually long-winded and detailed discussions of different kinds of pleasure and knowledge, which leads only at long last to the

---

1. When I speak of Socrates and the Socratic style of discussion I am referring to the portrait of Socrates in Plato's earlier dialogue, not the historic figure.

ultimate goal: selecting the ingredients of the good life. So what should persuade readers to expose themselves to such a troublesome journey? This gloomy picture of the dialogue's troublesome development will become considerably more cheerful if we take a bird's-eye view of its actual progression. For in spite of the many problems and the sheer amount of detail, Socrates seems confident about the strategy he pursues. The discussion starts with a clear exposition of the problem: How are pleasure and knowledge related to the human good? Is pleasure what makes our life a happy one, as *Philebus* and his friends hold, or is knowledge a better good, as Socrates maintains? The result of the discussion presents a precise answer to that question: Neither pleasure nor knowledge is assigned first prize in the contest, but a third thing is given that dignity, as Socrates had already vaguely envisaged at the beginning (11d–e). Indeed, not only does the end of the dialogue match the challenge at its beginning; Socrates never loses sight of where he is going. To arbitrate between the claims of pleasure and knowledge to supreme goodness, he regards it as necessary to distinguish between different kinds of pleasure and knowledge. Socrates obtains this concession not without a certain amount of resistance from his partner Protarchus' side. But once this resistance is overcome, Socrates convinces him of the need for a thorough review of the methodological problem the project entails: the problem of determining in what sense pleasure and knowledge are each a unitary phenomenon that contains a plurality. The question of the adequate method of dealing with this problem of the 'one and many' fills the whole first part of the dialogue, the part that I have referred to as 'purgatory'. It leads to a fourfold ontological classification of all things, which provides the basis for the ensuing determination of the nature of pleasure and knowledge, as well as for the lengthy critique of their various kinds. Once this critical evaluation is achieved, Socrates can turn to the final arbitration: 'Measure' and successful mixtures (what has measure) reach first and second place in this final ranking, reason and intelligence are assigned only third place, while the less purely intellectual endeavors obtain fourth place, and the few pure pleasures that slip through the critical evaluation hold fifth and last place on that list. This final judgment concludes the discussion to the satisfaction of both partners.

Such an overview should whet the Platonist's appetite. Except for the *Laws*, none of the other writings commonly recognized as forming the cluster of Plato's late dialogues discusses ethical questions in detail. But the review of the political order in the *Laws* is staged in faraway Crete, where there is no Socrates, and the ideas conceived for an ideal state are remote from Athenian life. If Plato in the *Philebus* returns late in his day to the most important ethics question—the highest good attainable in an individual life for the ordinary Athenian—and puts Socrates back center stage as his main spokesman, it must be of considerable interest for us to consider why he does so. For it stands to reason that Plato must have had urgent reasons for reviving the old controversy of 'pleasure vs. knowledge'. What adds to our interest is the very fact that he brings his sophisticated dialectical apparatus to bear on the decision over the good. Such an application promises to add considerably to our understanding of Plato's late dialectic. So the 'purgatory' of the *dialectico-metaphysical* part would seem to fulfill the function that a purgatory should serve, *viz.* to expurgate errors of understanding and to make us ready for a new assessment of the roles of pleasure and knowledge in human life, even if it should force us on a long march across a sometimes barren-looking plain before our final ascent to the true and the good.

However, if this bird's-eye view lightens up the gloomy picture by promising a well-directed and fruitful discussion, it has to be admitted that this is a very high-flying view. A low-flying bird will have quite a different perspective. What looks from very high up like a well-ordered landscape turns out, from close up, to be full of crags and ravines, bogs, and apparently unfordable rivers. So while the high-flyer's smooth general outline should not be forgotten (cf. the table of contents), we also have to take an inventory of the many difficulties that present themselves on a closer analysis of the text. A piecemeal treatment of the arguments in the different parts of the dialogue is needed to see what difficulties there are and how they are solved. Only then will the dialogue's coherence and the purpose of its detours emerge. A preview of its progress from the 'opening challenge' through its disparate two parts, the dialectico-metaphysical discourse and the critique of pleasure and knowledge, to the 'final ascent' to the true and the good, will give an idea of the discussion's inner unity and its ultimate results.

Helpful as such an integrative overview may be, it shares the dangers of all summaries of Platonic dialogues. There is, first and foremost, the temptation of presenting one's own line of interpretation as the dialogue's 'natural' purpose. It is easy to succumb to this temptation of 'streamlining' Plato, because of the need to present what he says as an integrated whole. Yet such a unifying interpretation may be grossly misleading, since it will present the dialogue as something it is not, namely, a philosophical treatise with a straightforward message. By reading it under some general assumptions of our own, we may completely miss Plato's intention. Possible alternatives to such a procedure are not enticing either, at least not when space is limited. It is appropriate neither to hand out a list of difficulties nor to confine the introduction to an impartial overview of the battlefield of conflicting opinions among the learned.[1] This introductory essay ought therefore to be treated as a very tentative general outline; questions about details will be left to the notes that accompany the text. It goes without saying that the acknowledgment of difficulties, indications of other possible interpretations, or discussions of other suggestions in the ample second-ary literature have to be kept at a minimum.

2. Analysis of the dialogue.
I. The introductory challenge:
pleasure vs. knowledge (11a–14b).

The opening scene of the dialogue is peculiar; we are introduced to an ongoing discussion at a moment where Socrates changes partners. The original protagonist of hedonism, Philebus, drops out, and his friend and admirer Protarchus becomes his spokesman. So hedonism throughout the dialogue is represented by *proxy*. This dramatic staging allows Plato to let Socrates begin with a summary of what allegedly preceded, so that the two positions about the good in human life have already 'congealed'.[2] The partners to the discussion have, for instance, already agreed that the human good is a state of the soul (11d) and not some external good such as wealth, beauty, or power.

What precisely is the bone of contention between the two parties? The *Phileban thesis* that pleasure is the good is couched in such terms that it allows for several interpretations. Philebus' thesis might be the *factual* claim that all creatures search for pleasure as their ultimate aim, or it might be the *normative* claim that all creatures ought to make the search for pleasure their ultimate aim. The text is open to both interpretations, but Socrates' final repetition of the two positions at 60a presents it as a normative thesis. There may also be the argument from 'nature's voice' at work here: What all creatures desire must be a natural good and hence will be desired by all. Another question concerns the exclusivity of the

---

1. Gosling's commentary (1975) on the *Philebus* does an admirable job of combining the apore-tic and synthetic modes of interpretation. The student is encouraged to consult it.

2. What further reasons may have prompted Plato to adopt this unusual opening will be discussed below.

claim. Does Philebus regard pleasure as the only good thing, or is it merely the best of many good things? The very vagueness of the initial formulation of his position should warn us not to narrow down that thesis unnecessarily. It seems to be deliberately presented as undifferentiated. Such a situation is familiar in Platonic dialogues. Socrates often has to deal with partners who do not know precisely what they think. By exposing the inconsistencies of their confused views, he forces them to make the necessary decisions about their views.

If the Phileban thesis that pleasure is the good is comprehensive but vague, the *Socratic position* is presented in a rather guarded way. Socrates does not claim that knowledge and all intellectual activities are the highest or the exclusive good. He merely calls knowledge a "better good than pleasure" and more profitable (11b). This leaves open the possibility that knowledge is neither the highest nor the only good. It also leaves room for compromise; thus Socrates can admit that knowledge provides man with some good other than itself, for the main feature of the good they are looking for is, in Socrates' words, that it should "render life happy" (11d6).

If Plato starts with two rival theses that clearly stand in need of further clarification and specification, this must mean that he does so deliberately. What alternatives to presenting pleasure and knowledge as the candidates for the highest good would there have been for him? He could have adopted the distinction of three types of goods that we find in Glaucon's challenge at the beginning of the second book of the *Republic*.[1] Such a move would have set up the discussion for a methodically much clearer start. If Plato does not take such a tack in the *Philebus*, he must have his reasons for not doing so. To be sure, Protarchus (and certainly Philebus) is no Glaucon. But since Socrates himself presents the alternatives, he could have done so in a more precise fashion. If Plato avoids the precision he might have sought at the outset, the most likely explanation for his procedure seems to be that he started with a vague formulation of the issues precisely because both pleasure and knowledge stand in need of further investigation. This is exactly what we will find confirmed in the dialogue's development. The *Philebus* seems designed as a thorough reinvestigation of the two ethically crucial concepts that, in different ways, Plato had already dealt with and played off against one another.

1. There are three kinds of goods, first the things that are regarded as goods in themselves, without any further considerations, such as life's harmless pleasures. Second, there are goods that are cherished both for their own sake and for the sake of their effects, such as knowledge, etc. Third, there are things that are taken to be good *only* for the sake of their effect, such as the painful exercises we submit to for the sake of health (*R.* 357b–d).

The opposition between pleasure and knowledge is indeed a *cause célèbre* in Plato. Their relationship is at stake as early as the *Protagoras*, where knowledge is made subservient to pleasure because knowledge is defined as the 'art of measuring' pleasure and pain (351b ff.). Knowledge reigns supreme in the *Gorgias*, when the necessity of a 'master art' for the selection of good and bad pleasures is demonstrated (499b ff.). Knowledge and pleasure are presented as candidates for the highest good in *Republic* VI (505b–d: Both are found wanting, for different reasons). And the relation between pleasure and knowledge is once again investigated in Book IX (580d ff.). Here we find a kind of truce forged between them: There are different pleasures in each of the three parts of the soul, and the philosopher's pleasures of the mind are the best and the greatest. As clear reminiscences in the *Philebus* show, Plato has not forgotten his earlier concern with the rivalry between pleasure and knowledge. What corrections or revisions he makes of his earlier views will emerge in the discussion. Picking up loose ends must certainly have been one of the aims he pursued in our dialogue.[1]

The trick of replacing the uncompromising hedonist Philebus by a proxy assures Socrates of a more cooperative partner in the common search for truth (11c8). But at first their cooperation threatens to fall apart over matters of principle. Even the more malleable Protarchus does not want to agree to the need for a *differentiation* among pleasures (12c–d). His reaction shows that he sees the importance of Socrates' move and suspects that it might load the dice against pleasure from the outset. So he insists on treating pleasure as a unitary phenomenon: What differences appear between various pleasures are due to the object or occasion of the pleasures, not to an opposition in their nature itself (12e1).

However, there is more to this denial of any distinction among pleasures on Protarchus' side than the dawning suspicion of a trap set by Socrates to force the concession that not all pleasures are equally good. A fundamental disagreement about the nature of pleasure is at work. Protarchus seems to identify pleasure with the feeling of elation, the 'kick'; as such, it is separable from its object or cause, a mere aftereffect or epiphenomenon, as we might say. The act of eating, for instance, is one process; its enjoyment is another. This conception has the advantage that all pleasures can be treated as equal; the only difference between them is a difference in *quantity*.[2]

---

1. For a more detailed discussion of the loose ends, see D. Frede (1985), esp. 151–161.

2. This is not to say that Protarchus clearly saw the implications of his position. An undifferentiated notion of pleasure as an immediate good suggests itself most easily for simple physical pleasures, especially since its counterpart, pain, is usually not regarded as tied to an object either.

For Socrates, as will gradually emerge in the dialogue, pleasure consists in the entire experience, including what we call the 'intentional object' of the enjoyment, i.e., what the pleasure is all about. He insists that there are *qualitative* distinctions among pleasures, including moral distinctions: There are things we ought not to enjoy. Socrates does not immediately argue for qualitative differences among pleasures; he first attacks the problem from a metaphysical point of view, by showing that generic unity is not incompatible with variety. All colors share one nature in being colors, but there are differences and even contrasts among them, as between black and white. This does not immediately settle the issue. For when Socrates tries to wrest from Protarchus the admission that the hedonists in fact call both good and bad pleasures equally good, Protarchus is not caught in this net: To admit that some pleasures are bad would mean to abandon his cause. He retreats once again to the position that pleasures cannot be opposed to one another insofar as they are pleasures. At this point the discussion threatens to become deadlocked, a deadlock that is overcome only by a somewhat exasperated appeal from Socrates: If they want to make progress they should agree to the need to make distinctions, both the party that favors pleasure and the party that favors intelligence. This appeal works. Protarchus is persuaded that nothing bad can happen to his theory as long as the other side is in the same boat (14a). As we shall see, this turns out to be the most important concession on the hedonist's side in the dialogue.

Should Protarchus have given in so easily? That depends on the seriousness of his conviction of the homogeneity of pleasure. If he refused to accept Socrates' argument merely for fear of its consequences for his position, then he was right to give up his resistance. If he found the analogy with colors or shapes unconvincing, he should have put up a fight against it. Such a move (difficult to argue anyway) does not seem to have occurred to him, so he is open to Socrates' appeal not to block progress because of blind partisanship (14b5 *philonikia*). Protarchus agrees, so the basic plurality of pleasure and knowledge is taken as established. The first chink is thus broken off the hedonist's armor; a systematic investigation can begin.

II. The "dialectical" part of the dialogue: problems of classification and division (14b–31b).

The next task Socrates sets up is to determine the kind of unity and plurality that can be assigned to pleasure and knowledge. But instead of attacking this question directly, he first teaches his audience to appreciate the problem of *unity and plurality* in general. This turns into a long lecture on the method of division (14b–20a), whose point in the dialogue is prima facie unclear, because it does not lead to the result one would expect. Socrates does not harvest the fruits of his labor but suddenly declares that they can dispense with such a division after all! The goodness of pleasure and knowledge can be determined in a simpler fashion (20b). Because of this seeming lack of coherence, some commentators have suspected that Plato inserted a general excursion on the method of dialectic here, without much concern for its integration in the text.[1] As we will see later, this claim is not justified; there is more intrinsic unity than first meets the eye, although it may well also be true that Plato was looking for an opportunity to say more about his method of division in general.

II.1. The problem of "the One and the Many" and the method of dialectic (14b–20a).

The occasion for such a general lecture is provided by Protarchus' lack of comprehension of the question of unity and plurality. He does not see that the suggested analogy of pleasure and knowledge with the unity and plurality of color and shape (12e–13a) would be a differentiation among *kinds*. Instead he thinks of the plurality constituted by the different properties in an *individual*. Socrates rebukes Protarchus for this misunderstanding: This problem of plurality is "too commonplace and childish" to be taken seriously any longer. The severity of Socrates' correction not only surprises Protarchus but must also surprise the attentive reader of Plato's earlier dialogues; for the problem of how things can have conflicting properties, so that they are large and small, heavy and light at the same time, is one which he had not always regarded as child's play. It is taken seriously in the *Phaedo*, where it is regarded as one of the difficulties that must be settled for and by the theory of the Forms (102a ff.). It recurs in the *Republic* (523e–525a) and is still deemed worthy of attention in the *Theaetetus* (154c). So what is the reason for Socrates' snobbishness here? It seems that the Socrates of the *Philebus* has internalized the declaration of his courageous younger self in the *Parmenides* about the innocuousness of such alleged paradoxes (*Parm.* 127e–130a): There is nothing surprising if individual things participate in different properties; it would be amazing, however, if the Forms themselves did so. Young Socrates then gets an

---

1. Cf. Striker, 9.

unforgettable lecture about the difficulties of handling the Forms from Master Parmenides himself.

Socrates' refusal to take seriously the old problems of unity and plurality is not the only reminder of the *Parmenides* in the *Philebus*. The ensuing explanation of the *real problem* is full of allusions to that debate. Not only does Socrates now shift the discussion from individual sensible things to a discussion of the Forms; the problems, the terminology, and even the examples he uses here are largely the same that Parmenides brought up against Forms in the debate with Socrates' younger self.[1] Unfortunately the text presents us with problems here (15a–b) that have caused quite a controversy about the precise nature of the difficulties Plato has in mind. The question is whether the passage 15b1–c3 contains *three* problems concerning the Forms, as the punctuation in the Oxford edition suggests, or whether there are only *two* questions, as I have assumed in my translation (following the lead of many other scholars). We have to take a closer look at what is at stake.

Questions one and three are at least clear in their intention: The *first* problem Socrates addresses is whether the assumed units or monads ought to be accepted as having *true being*, such as Man and Ox, the Good and the Beautiful.[2] The *third* question raises the problem of *how* the Forms can possess both unity in themselves and plurality in their many instantiations that undergo generation and destruction. Socrates indicates that neither of two options seems feasible here: The Form cannot be dispersed and become many, nor can it remain one and become "entirely separated from itself" in the process.[3]

No such relative clarity obtains as far as the alleged *second* question about the Forms is concerned: "Then again how they are supposed to be, whether each one of them is always one and the same, admitting neither

---

1. In both dialogues the 'real problem' of the one and many is called "amazing" (*thaumaston, Parm.*129a–e; *Phil.* 14c) or even "monstrous" (*teras, Parm.* 129b2; *Phil.* 14e3). The Good and the Beautiful are examples used in both dialogues, as is Man; but while Socrates expressed doubt about man and other natural entities in the *Parmenides*, in the *Philebus*, Man and Ox are treated as no more problematic than the other cases.

2. Although the question is clear, it is answered only indirectly; the 'divine gift', dialectical method, shows that its objects have generic or specific unity. This kind of unity seems sufficient for our dialogue. Much later Socrates also mentions 'divine' ideal mathematical objects, but no information is given about the extension of that class, whether there is such a thing as 'divine man' or 'divine ox'.

3. These difficulties also echo the problems that Parmenides had raised for young Socrates to shake his faith in the separability of the Forms (131a ff.).

of generation nor of destruction, but is nonetheless most certainly this one" (15b2–3). The trouble with this question is to see why there should be any difficulty with the everlasting unities at all. If anything could be unproblematically *one*, it should be the supertemporal Forms. Now there is no dearth of possible cures for the text or of tacitly understood supplements that would make it a question worth asking.[1] The most natural supplement would be the assumption that Plato is somehow referring to the fact that the Forms as *genera* are wholes with parts. This would connect both with what preceded and with what is to follow, for the subsequent elucidation of the question of the 'one and many' is concerned with the division of genera into species. The problem with this assumption is that there is no indication of it whatever in the text. It would have been easy for Plato to make clear that the second question is how the Forms can be one *and many* on the level of the unchangeable. That there is no indication of this important point at all must weigh heavily against justifying it as a tacit understanding. Moreover, the examples of Forms are not well-chosen if Plato had counted on such a tacit understanding. For while the good and the beautiful can be taken as containing subgenera (thereby being many), no such plurality can hold for the Forms of man or ox.

There remains the possibility that Plato is referring to the difficulty of *knowing* the Forms in and of themselves, which he also addresses in the *Parmenides*, once under the perspective that the Forms are in a region by themselves and only open to Knowledge itself, not to *our* knowledge (133b–134c), and again, under the perspective of the *austerity* of the Forms: If they are just what they are, how can we ever address them *as* anything, even as *one*, as the *same*, or give them a name (cf. the first hypothesis, 137c–142a)? The problem with this assumption is, once again, that there is no indication in the text that Plato has anything like it in mind. For in that case he ought to have phrased the alleged second question differently and not already presupposed that each Form is securely one and the same at 15b2–3. There is no indication here that the 'unknowability' or the 'austerity' of the Forms is the problem. For this reason—though somewhat reluctantly, in view of the strained reading of the Greek it presupposes—I have adopted the two-question interpretation. Thus we are left with two problems: first, whether Forms ought to be assumed at all; and second, what kind of status they have, whether eternally selfsame when taken by themselves, or also dispersed and multiplied in the sensible world.

1. For a fuller discussion cf. Gosling (1975), 143 ff.; R. Dancy (1984).

Whether we assume two questions here or three, however, we still have the most important problem on our hands, namely, whether and how the Socrates of the *Philebus* actually solves these questions. This problem is all the more important, because he adds that it makes all the difference whether or not they are properly settled (15c2–3). In the text that immediately follows, this problem is addressed in what is at best an oblique fashion. Neither the *diagnosis* Socrates gives at first about what causes the problem (15d–16a) nor his subsequent recommendation of a *cure* by a "divine method" (16b–17a) seem prima facie clearly related to the problems of the Forms as he addressed them in the previous passage on their unity and plurality. So we have to take a closer look at what the diagnosis diagnoses and what the cure cures.

To take up first the problems with the *diagnosis*: Socrates seems to suggest that it is inescapable that unities become many when we *talk* about them ("they flit around . . ."). This inescapable condition is exploited by naughty boys who enjoy involving anyone they can get hold of in confusion. So there is a real problem with unity, which becomes a mess in the hands of naughty boys. What unities is he talking about here? What is it that the naughty boys do? And what does it have to do with Forms? The text does not tell us. But since Socrates claims that the problem is a general one which comes to us inescapably when we speak (not only to philosophers and naughty boys), he is likely referring to the fact that in all statements something *else* is attributed to the subject, so that its unity becomes doubtful. We may say of Socrates, for instance, that he is a man or an animal. But he is not the only man or animal. How can Socrates be one thing if he shares this name (and nature) with many others which are not man or animal in the same sense? If Socrates is not the same man as Plato or the same animal as Fido, the question is in what sense he can *be* what he is said to be, *viz.* man or animal. Must not such an attribution immediately pluralize the subject? If this assumption about the kind of condition that "comes through discourse" is correct, we can see why Plato calls it "immortal and ageless": As long as we speak we have to live with that question, whether we are aware of it or not. And Plato may have assumed that this problem must become explicit sooner or later, whenever humankind reflects. Whether or not we assume separate Forms, we have a problem with general predicates.

The discovery of this plurality of common names is what the naughty boys exploit: "moving every statement, at one point turning it all into one, and then again dividing things up" (15e–16a). The naughty boys might argue, for instance, that if man is (an) animal and ox is animal, then man

is ox. They might also argue for the reverse: If man and ox are different
animals, then there is no such thing as 'animal' but an infinity of animals,
so that man and ox might be anything at all. Thus the multiplicity of
meaning can be used to "spread things out"; one and the same thing
cannot without contradiction be called one, while for the opposite approach
different things can all be collapsed in one. In the hands of the boys the
"ageless and immortal condition" becomes a sheer nuisance, because they
play around with linguistic ambiguities without quite knowing what they
are doing ("involving both themselves and everyone else in confusion").
That boys should not have access to dialectic, because they misuse
it and take it as a kind of sport where victory is all that counts, is mentioned
in the *Republic* (539b). Examples of types of arguments that exploit possible and impossible double meanings of terms and the confusion they
cause are extensively displayed in Plato's *Euthydemus*, where two sophistic
clowns enmesh even Socrates with such gimmicks.[1] In this way problems
of the 'one and many' formed the basis of the sophists' business. The
sophistic background of our passage in the *Philebus* is confirmed by Protarchus' reaction. As his mock-threat against Socrates (16a) shows, he understands quite well that Socrates is alluding to some common or garden
variety of juvenile word-play. The problem with such 'equivocity' of language thus turns out to have both a serious side that needs to be taken
care of and a fun side that will fall by the wayside once the serious problem
is taken care of.[2]

So far this diagnosis of the problem of 'the one and many' does not
bring the partners closer to a solution. In fact it seems only to widen the
problem's scope, because it turns out not to be confined to the recondite
theory of the Forms, but shows up in all discourse. That such a widening
of the scope is indeed the purpose of the discussion of the alleged equivocity of language is confirmed by the way in which Socrates introduces
the *cure* for the condition, in response to his partner's complaint that he
should clear up the confusion. Socrates is unusually careful and solemn
about the "finer way" that is to help them out of their difficulties, when

1. As the *Sophist* shows, serious philosophers were troubled by the wizardry of language too.
The so-called late learners held the theory that each thing can only be named by its own
name, because all other attributes must be alien to it (*Sph.* 251b). So language would have
to be restricted to identity statements such as "man is man," "good is good."

2. Whether this reconstruction does justice to Plato's intentions must remain a moot point.
But it seems to connect best with the preceding problem of the multiplicity of the Forms
and the subsequent explanation of the method of dialectic.

he announces it as a method that he "always admired, although it often left him stranded." He even claims divine origin for it: It has been hurled down like lightning from heaven by some Prometheus to teach mankind the method of all scientific enterprise.

What is this method? The clue comes at the end of Socrates' long explanation, when he mentions that its proper exercise is the practice of *dialectic*, while its misuse is mere *eristic*, the hallmark of the sophists' art (17a5). But why is Socrates so modest here about his own relation to this method? That Socrates should refuse to take credit for an important thought is nothing unusual. There are many occasions where he attributes decisive moves to other authorities; we have only to recall the priests and priestesses in the *Meno* (81a), or Diotima's lecture in the *Symposium* (201c). Common opinion has it that through such devices Plato is indicating where he lets his Socrates go beyond the historical Socrates' teaching. However, the method of dialectic is not something Plato's Socrates is shy of using elsewhere. In earlier dialogues he repeatedly recommended and discussed it, at least in outline, without any such compunction (cf. *R.* 532a– 534e; *Phdr.* 266b). The overall schema of dialectic, as recommended here, of *collection* into a generic unity and *division* into the species is familiar from the *Phaedrus* on. We find ample examples of such divisions in the *Sophist* and the *Politicus*, and warning is repeatedly given that they must be performed in a methodical way.[1]

What new element justifies the dramatic invocation of a 'divine' origin for this method here? Socrates presents it with a new twist by prescribing a more rigorous shape to collections and divisions. Its novelty is also emphasized by a new terminology, the introduction of the concepts of 'limit' (*peras*) and 'unlimitedness' (*apeiria*). How are they applied and in this application what constitutes an increased rigor? The rigor consists in the demand for numerically exact subdivisions of the highest genus into species and subspecies until the ultimate specifications have been reached, which do not allow for any further proper division. Only after the numerically precise account of the members ('limit') has been achieved on each level can the division come to an end. Only then is it right to concede an unlimited multitude of the many instances. Fortunately Plato does not confine himself to this highly abstract schema but gives some examples

---

1. There is the famous passage in the *Phaedrus* where Socrates warns of divisions by hack-cooks who don't know the natural joints, 265d–6b. The difficulties of dividing are also commented on extensively in the *Politicus*, and the many divisions in the *Sophist* where Socrates is not the speaker, of course, are clearly an illustration of these difficulties.

for its application. The first example concerns the field of linguistics and writing, the second that of music. There is some doubt whether Socrates has two or three examples in mind, because he first discusses the unity and plurality of letters, then that of the sounds of music, and finally tells the story of the discovery of letters by the Egyptian god Theuth, as if it were yet another example. But it seems clear that the story of Theuth is a supplement to the first example.

What exactly do the exemplifications of the divine method show? Although the precise interpretation of these examples presents difficulties, Plato's overall intention seems clear enough. If we take together the two passages that deal with the art of writing (17a–b and 18b–d), the following picture emerges: The art of writing would never have been discovered if mankind had rested content with merely observing that the sounds that we articulate are a unitary phenomenon with an unlimited range of instances and varieties. The discovery of writing depended on the systematic and complete division of the elements of speech; first into vowels and consonants, with the sounded consonants in the middle; and then into their respective species, the different kinds of letters that represent the sounds. This order and structure was the great discovery that Socrates attributes to the Egyptian god Theuth.[1] It was Theuth who put *order* into the unlimited variety of spoken sound and established its different kinds (vowels, consonants, and semiconsonants) and the species of letters they contain. This enabled him to establish "letter" as the unifying supreme genus and to show what kind of a unity it forms. No one can claim knowledge in this field who does not know precisely how many species and subspecies there are.

The example of music is less easy to understand. First, the music of the Greeks is very different from ours; their scales do not coincide with ours (the Greeks permit units smaller than half-tones and a greater variety of scales), and the major and minor modes in our classical music do not sufficiently illustrate the rich variety of the modes in Greek music. Furthermore, Plato himself is rather vague about the details of the music example. His first division of musical sounds, "high and low and even," has caused confusion, because this trichotomy does not seem to carve out

---

1. On the Egyptian god of writing, cf. the article "Thoth" in Pauly-Wissowa *RE* VI A 1, 351–388. On the Greeks and literacy in general, cf. Rhys Carpenter, "The Antiquity of the Greek Alphabet," *American Journal of Archeology*, 37 (1933); J. Naveh, *The Early History of the Alphabet*, Jerusalem and Leiden, 1982.

natural segments at all, but rather points up an unclear relative distinction: In reference to any given note, every other note will be either higher, lower, or of the same pitch. This looks like a quite arbitrary division, so commentators have doubted that it is division in the technical sense at all.[1]

If one considers the origin of that trichotomy and the technical background of Plato's musical theory, however, this impression of arbitrariness disappears. The complex Greek system took its origin from the simple three-stringed lyre with the lowest note (*hypate*), the middle (*mese*), and the last or highest (*neate*).[2] This simple schema was altered almost beyond recognition as Greek music developed and became organized in *tetrachords*, i.e., units of four notes each, where two tetrachords form an octave. The primitive tripartition did not disappear entirely, however, but gave its name to the high, middle, and low tetrachords. In that more elaborate system, each note is defined by the interval it forms with the highest note of its tetrachord. Further specifications become complicated, because the intervals within the tetrachords are not fixed but vary with the *mode* of a piece of music. These modes determine the "character of the intervals, by what notes they are defined, and the kinds of combinations they form," as Plato indicates (17d). One and the same musical sound can be part of a different mode and scale, so that it may appear under a different name in different modes, or appear in one mode but not in another. Here at least we can point to an analogy with our musical system. The same notes have different functions on different scales. F# is part of both the A-major and the D-major scale (it is the sixth in the first, the third in the latter), but it does not occur in A minor or D minor.

As his use of technical terminology in the *Republic* shows (443d), Plato could very well have been more explicit in his explanations in the *Philebus*. If he avoids explanation, he must have counted on the understanding of every educated Greek.[3] From Protarchus' reaction we can see that he needs no further enlightenment. To more systematically divide the ele-

---

1. Striker, 25–30. For a more detailed discussion of these issues, cf. G. Löhr (1990), 101–188.

2. The terms *hypate* ("upmost") for the lowest and *neate/nete* ("last") for the highest refers to their position relative to the player, not their pitch.

3. In connection with the later 'fourfold division of being' it will become clear that Socrates has a further reason for not adopting the technical vocabulary: He wants to maintain a close parallel between music and other things that belong to the "mixed class," where the limit that is imposed on the unlimited provides stability and harmony. The "unlimited" in music is the "high and the low," "the fast and the slow" (26a).

ments of music in all its details would have been a time-consuming and cumbersome enterprise.[1]

This brief outline must suffice as a rough indication of how the dialectical method combines the unity and plurality of its subject matter and how it treats every object of study as an integral whole. Two questions will present themselves to the reader at this point. First, we want to know why Socrates professes to have difficulties with this method, if, as he says, it is the traditional method of all science. Second, what answer, if any, does this method provide for the problems of the unity and plurality of the Forms themselves, which Socrates had indicated in the crucial passage at 15a–b? In what sense is the "heavenly method" a *cure* for the difficulties?

Taking the first question first, one of Socrates' difficulties must certainly lie in the *completeness* of the divisions. How are we to know that we have found *all* natural subdivisions? Then there is the problem of establishing the highest genus as a *unity*. There is also the problem of determining whether the actual divisions are genuine, i.e., *natural*, divisions and not arbitrarily imposed. That these difficulties are serious is confirmed by a study of the practice of divisions in Plato, most prominently in the series of divisions in the *Sophist* or the *Politicus*. The student cannot help wondering what justifies the order of these divisions and the criteria for their selection. There is no direct answer to this question, nor can there likely be one; the criteria for the method's proper application are up to the expert in each field. The philosopher is limited to clarifying the general schema and insisting on strict numerical control, whether the scientist proceeds from the genus via the species to the unlimited multitude of the instances ("top down") or, by force of circumstances, from the unlimited multitude to the highest genus ("bottom up"). So the critical scientist will have to ask how many kinds are on each level and whether and why there should be these and only these. The important issue is that there should be no omissions. This, Socrates concludes, is the method by which the gods want us to do research, to learn, and to teach each other. That he calls it a venerable tradition does not mean it has been consciously and conscien-

---

1. To suggest an analogy, we might call all notes above a′, "high" and all those below it "low" and characterize every existing note as a member of its mode (e.g., upper f# in G major, or in D major or in E minor). Since in Greek music the note in each mode is defined by its position in the tetrachord, its relative position can be used to characterize a particular note ("two full steps down").

tiously observed by mankind all along. He finds his contemporaries delinquent in that respect: They do not proceed methodically but skip the important 'middle part' in their divisions and therefore do not really practice dialectic but remain on the level of mere eristic argumentation.

Is the same deficiency the cause of the mess produced by the naughty boys? That may very well be what Socrates has in mind. If strict procedure is observed, fallacies based on linguistic vagueness will no longer be possible. It would not be possible to conclude that if man is (an) animal and ox is animal, then man and ox are one and the same, because the intermediate steps would determine what *kinds* of animals man and ox are, and how they differ. The solution for distinctions among individuals would depend on how Plato would settle what it means to be a member of an unlimited multitude that shares a species. Whatever the principle of individuation may be, a simple equation would no longer be available for the boys' sport if being a man is now spelled out in terms of sharing a common type.

This leaves us with the second question, what *cure* the divine method provides for the problem of the unity or multiplicity of the Forms. Does the divine method contain a solution, or has the whole question been sidestepped? If the divine method is meant to be as widely applied as Socrates seems to suggest (16c9), clearly it must also apply to the Forms. One can go even further and claim that Plato should be understood to say that it applies *primarily* to the Forms, if the genera and species are Forms. What speaks in favor of conceiving them as Forms? The description of the divine method suggests that genera and species are unchangeable entities; the genus animal, for instance, is the nature common to all animals, and this common nature is *invariable* and *one*. It does not come to be nor does it pass away with individual animals. What it is to be an animal or a human being remains always the same, regardless of how and when animality or humanity is instantiated. If the Forms are conceived in this 'scientific way' neither their unity nor their plurality is problematic any longer; the situation as envisaged at 15a–b does not obtain. There is not the Form itself in splendid isolation in the realm of the eternal, and a hopeless multitude of the Forms split up and dispersed in the realm of generation and destruction. If this interpretation is correct, the earlier diagnosis of the way in which Forms are one and many was mistaken and is now revised. The Form *qua* Form remains a unity despite the fact that it always already contains integral parts: It admits a *limited plurality* insofar as it is specifiable in terms of its species and subspecies; and it admits the possibility of *unlimited plurality*, since there can be an unlimited number of animals. Each Form, then, represents a unity and plurality on several levels. There is generic unity, and there is specific unity, and there is the unity of the sensible object that is a member of the species and genus. There is a limited specific plurality, and there is unlimited plurality among the sensible objects. None of those pluralities is any threat to the generic or specific unity as such.

The question of the unity of a Form finds its answer in the application of the divine method, which ensures that *all* specific parts have been found and properly labeled.[1] The only worry for the practitioner of dialectic in each field lies in ensuring the completeness and appropriateness of the divisions. This is why Socrates stresses the importance of that procedure: We do not understand any of its parts unless we understand the whole (18c–d). It is not possible to understand the nature of a musical note in general, or how to identify a particular note, unless the whole system is properly demarcated. That otherwise no mastery can be achieved in any field is solemnly affirmed by Socrates once again (19b): "Unless we are able to do this for every kind of unity, similarity, sameness, and their opposites, in the way that our recent discussion has indicated, none of us will ever turn out to be any good at anything."

This cure for the problem of the unity and plurality of the Forms through scientific accuracy and systematic completeness will surprise only those among Plato's admirers who do not take seriously his often repeated demand for correct dialectic procedure. Only in the *Philebus*, however, does he work out at greater length what he usually only hints at when he refers to the music or writing master's skills and to the proper treatment of sounds and letters, the basic entities (*stoicheia*) of their art.[2]

After this dramatic buildup in presenting the only scientifically correct way to deal with any problem whatsoever, one next expects to see the dialectic method applied to pleasure and knowledge respectively. But equally dramatically, this is not what happens. When Protarchus declares himself incapable of performing this arduous task and entreats Socrates to do it for them or to find some other solution, Socrates takes the second option and sidesteps the issue of divisions with the plea that a sudden recollection of a dream, conveniently sent by some divinity, makes such an exertion superfluous, after all.

---

1. This does not mean that there are no problems with the application of the method. Problems exist, but they concern the expert in each field, not the metaphysician.

2. For a further discussion of this issue cf. D. Frede (1989), 20–49.

II.2. Socrates' dream: a compromise solution (20b–23b).

Much as we are used to appeals to dreamlike recollections on Socrates' part, this sudden brainstorm must take us by surprise, even if he claims some kind of divine interference as his excuse.[1] For this dramatic change forces us to question whether the long passage on dialectic and methodology is relevant for the dialogue's own topic, the arbitration between pleasure and knowledge. Did Plato insert it in the text because he needed *some* opportunity to divulge his new 'arithmetically rigorous' method of division? In that case, he could not have done a worse job at integrating it in the text, from a dramatic point of view, when he turns away from it abruptly with the help of a *deus ex machina*. Nothing could be more conspicuous than this change of topic. If we do not want to settle for such compositional fumbling on Plato's part, we need a more appropriate explanation to save the dialogue's inner unity. Such an explanation will indeed appear when we come to a closer analysis of the 'fourfold ontological division' that follows Socrates' dream. So it is best to postpone that question and first take inventory of the compromise solution that is the result of that dream.

The 'new solution' that supposedly facilitates the decision of the contest between pleasure and knowledge looks at first like a quick fix. Socrates "remembers" that neither of the two are the good, and a third thing is better than either of the two; the contest is thus reduced to a decision over the silver medal. That neither of the two contestants deserves first prize is established by a kind of litmus test. Anything that is unqualifiedly *the Good* good must fulfill three conditions. It must be complete (*teleion*), sufficient (*hikanon*), and desired as such by all who know it (*ephietai* 20d). How is this triad justified? It seems that there is no further justification; Socrates must be counting on the fact that few people would actually reject these conditions for the good. His strategy has in fact changed at this point: His partner's consent is the decisive factor. This change in style and scope is easy to explain: They have returned to their old topic, the good in human life; if the result of their investigation is to have any force, his partner must agree to it. So Protarchus is to determine whether a life of pleasure without any kind of knowledge or a life of knowledge without any pleasure fulfills the three criteria. Common human insight rather than a divine method decides the question here.

But if Protarchus is to speak for common sense, he must first be weaned

---

1. Most famous is Socrates' Dream in the *Theaetetus* (201d–e), but he appeals to dreams elsewhere as well.

of his naive assumption that a life of pleasure, pure and simple, fulfills the three criteria. This weaning is achieved by a brief but successfull *elenchus*, the only refutation as such in our dialogue. When Socrates points out that a life of pleasure without any kind of intellectual capacity condemns the hedonist to the mindless life of a mollusk, Protarchus admits that he is reduced to speechlessness (*aphasia*, 21d). Should Protarchus have conceded defeat so easily? Commentators have sometimes objected that it is unfair of Socrates to abstract all awareness from pleasure, as if even bare awareness of pleasure had to be a kind of intellectual activity. But such an objection would not have gotten Protarchus very far. Any self-respecting hedonist would want more than the bare recognition of pleasant feelings at the moment they happen. If there is to be anything worth calling a *human life*, there has to be memory of past pleasures and full comprehension of present and possible future ones. Protarchus' reaction shows that he sees the point. Moreover, the fact that knowledge does not fare any better than unmitigated hedonism makes it easier for him to abandon the argument; a life containing a mixture of pleasure and knowledge is clearly superior to a life of pleasure or knowledge only.

As far as dramatic development is concerned, the dialogue has here reached its turning point. Protarchus is no longer the spokesman of hedonism. The surrender has actually taken place in two stages. At first Protarchus surrendered the discussion to Socrates as far as the *method* was concerned. He accepted the need to apply the 'divine method' but saw himself as incapable of doing so. Now he realizes that he can no longer function as pleasure's advocate: The mixed life is a better good. So he appeals to Socrates to carry on the search for it. The investigation has turned into a joint project, despite the fact that Protarchus still hopes for some place of honor for pleasure (22e). Philebus' angry interruption (22c) shows that he recognizes the importance of that change: The case of unmitigated hedonism has been abandoned by its appointed spokesman.

If the change in Protarchus' position from adversary to collaborator is clear, it may nevertheless come as a surprise that Socrates himself seems partisan to this compromise and gives up his role as champion of knowledge. That he has no reservations about doing so can be seen from the way he 'finalizes' the need for a mixed life: All creatures would prefer such a life; any disagreement would be due either to ignorance or to some unfortunate circumstance (later in the dialogue we will learn more about such a case, cf. 44b ff.). The loophole he might seem to leave for reason in his assent to the preference for a mixed life concerns only the *divine* reason (22c). A *human* life, he asserts once again without reservation, is better if it is a mixture of the two competing goods. The reasons for Socrates' willingness to compromise will emerge more clearly when the final selection of ingredients for the good life is at stake.

II.3. The fourfold division of all beings (23b–27c).

If Socrates' dream and the compromise of a mixed life promise to shorten the discussion, this is a short-lived hope. The decision whether the silver medal should be given to pleasure or to knowledge turns into a protracted investigation with its own demands. First of all, Socrates claims, a new kind of division is necessary whose purpose and relation to the previous one, the 'divine method', is far from clear. Among the many problematic details in this part of the text, the most worrisome is Socrates' initial announcement that they have to make "partial use of the old armament" they had previously applied (23b). If such a 'partial use' can be substantiated, then the inherent unity of the dialogue will be vindicated against the sceptics, for it would mean that the divine method was indeed designed for further use in the dialogue, in spite of Socrates' seeming about-face. At first sight things don't look encouraging, however. The fourfold division of "all beings" that Socrates now undertakes seems only distantly related to the 'divine method'. The employment of "limit" (*peras*) and "unlimited" (*apeiron*) in both passages does not mend matters. In fact it appears to make matters worse, for the terms seem to be used in quite different ways in both passages. So what is the point of the pretended similarity? Does Plato want to give the appearance of more coherence than is actually warranted?

Let us first take a look at this new division of "everything that actually exists now in the universe" (23c) before we return to the question of coherence. Since Socrates introduces it with such a flourish, we should take him at his word and assume that he means what he says, *viz.* that the division into four kinds is, at least for his present purposes, the ontologically most general division there can be. Whether it literally contains 'all there is' has to be left open for the time being. The four kinds are the unlimited, the limit, the mixture of the limit and the unlimited, and finally the cause of such mixtures. To get over the first bewilderment at this unprecedented division, let us take a quick look at its specifications for the four kinds and at some of the examples.

The first class, the *unlimited*, contains all things that have no definite measure or degree in themselves. As examples we find 'the hot' and 'the cold', but somewhat to our confusion, also the 'hotter' and 'the colder' and everything else 'in which the more and less reside', the dryer and wetter, faster and slower. There is even room for excess: There can be 'very much' or 'too much' of such unlimited things (24e–25a). Given all these specifications, many commentators have assumed that this class of beings signifies different kinds of *continua*, such as the continuum of temperature in the case of the hotter and the colder. But this assumption does not match well with Socrates' claim that these entities are in constant flux until they take on a definite quantity when they come to a standstill. This cannot apply to the continuum itself, if it represents the whole spectrum, for that cannot suddenly take on a definite degree and go out of existence, nor can it be in flux itself.[1] What can be in flux is only an item of a certain kind, a 'hot thing' that can vacillate in temperature and still be a hot thing until it accepts a limit and thereby stops floating around. So the preferable solution is to regard the *apeira* as the kinds of things that have no definite degree in themselves.

The second class, the *limit*, is defined as what imposes a definite degree or quantity (*poson*) on what is in itself unlimited. Plato is rather vague as to the exact nature of the limit, but the reason for this vagueness soon becomes apparent. The limit determines the right balance between the opposed unlimited elements that make up a harmonious mixture; whether the limit is an arithmetical proportion or a relation between geometric extensions or between intensive magnitudes depends on the kinds of elements. Wherever we say that something is 'just right', the quantitative relation among the ingredients is the limit. Because the right limit depends on the kind of thing that is to have a limit, Plato claims that the 'collection' of the limit into one genus will become clearer once the other two kinds, i.e., *mixture* and its *cause*, have been elucidated (25d). As will emerge, not just any kind of arithmetical or geometrical relation constitutes a limit of the kind Plato is talking about here.

The third class contains the *mixtures* of the limit and the unlimited. What kinds of entities are these? Since the unlimited is said to be in permanent flux (24d), one might expect the mixed class to contain all things that have a definite degree or extension. But this assumption seems to be wrong. Plato's examples and further specifications indicate that only *good* mixtures form that third class, such as fine weather, beauty, strength, and the virtues in the soul (26a–b). Only entities that contain a commensu-

1. For a fuller discussion of this issue, cf. Striker, 42–50.

rate or harmonious mixture of opposed elements seem to belong in this class.

Finally, there is the fourth class, the *cause* (*aitia*) of the mixtures (26e). Although it seems at first as if any kind of cause that leads to a mixture would be contained in that class, Socrates' later elucidation of it seems to show that it is made up exclusively by reason, both divine and human (30b–c). This restriction also confirms the assumption that the mixed class is confined to successful mixtures, like health, whose cause is a form of reason since it is the product of the art of medicine. Plato seems to assume that only reason can be the cause of such harmonious states, whether divine or human.

If this summary fairly represents Plato's overall rationale for this classi-fication, the details stand in need of further elucidation. In particular, the restriction of the mixed class leaves us in a bit of a quandary that affects our understanding of the whole fourfold classification. What about all those things to which we would ascribe a *definite quantity* but that are not good or successful mixtures? What about heat of 95° Fahrenheit or a frost of minus 4°? And what about my quite definite personal degree of avarice and sloth? Or does Plato assume that such states are forever in flux, so that he would simply deny that imperfect states can ever have definite degrees? Since Plato in other dialogues often supports a Heracli-tean flux for the world of the senses, it would not be surprising if that was his presupposition here.

Plato's extensive description of the class of the unlimited suggests that his main point is not the old saw about the permanent flux of all material entities. His explanation of inherent unlimitedness concerns not only specific states of sensible entities or qualities but also their genera and species, in which no definite degree at one point of time is feasible. Of course *my* fever right now will have its definite degree, as does *my* avarice or the present cold wave. But such entities have no intrinsic degree *qua* fever, avarice, or frost. They could have other degrees and still be fever, avarice, and a cold wave. I could be extremely stingy or just an ordinary penny-pincher; it could be frightfully cold outside or just slightly below average; a feverish person could be delirious or just suffer from a mild fever of 101.3°F. None of those variations would alter the fact that it is cold outside, even too cold, or that I am feverish or avaricious. This is the reason why 'the more and less' is the common characteristic of these entities. Anything that can retain its *identity* through a change in quantity belongs to this category. With the good mixtures this is not so. They are either 'just right' or not good mixtures at all. Health, fine climate, and the virtue of liberality presuppose a definite degree of their constituents. There can be no vacillation in these cases. The degree they have is not accidental or momentary but fixed once and for all in their very nature! Any deviation would mean that they are no longer the proper mixtures they are supposed to be. Are there other mixtures besides good ones? Plato mentions later in the dialogue that a mixture without proportion is only "an unconnected medley" (64d–e). When no limit is imposed on the ingredients, the inherent lack of measure in the medley itself prevents them from being stable and harmonious mixtures.

The lack of measure in the unlimited also explains the puzzling variety of its members. The *apeiron* contains not only the opposite qualities themselves (the hot and the cold, the dry and the wet) but also the corresponding relatives (hotter and colder, faster and slower) as well as other modifications (mildly hot) or excesses (very hot, too hot).[1] The explanation for Plato's 'generosity' is that such qualities allow for relativity, exaggeration, and change while remaining what they are. When something is hot, its heat may be hotter than something else's or hotter than it was before. Depending on the context, we may call it very hot or too hot or only mildly hot. None of these specifications applies to the harmonious mixtures: If health is a state of perfection, its possessor cannot be more or less healthy, nor too healthy, nor only mildly healthy. If we sometimes use such expressions, then it is a sloppy way of speaking. We illegitimately treat health as analogous to its counterpart, sickness. Sickness is an *apeiron*; it allows for differences of degree, relativity, and other such specifications. I can be mildly ill or violently ill, but it is wrong to project those specifications onto health, properly understood.

Right mixtures, then, always have a definite nature. What constitutes their goodness, apart from the fact that Socrates calls them harmonious? The common denominator of his examples, *viz.* health, strength, the seasons, music, and virtue, is that there is an *orderliness* and purpose to all of them. Is the mixed class limited to entities where the very name itself implies a kind of perfection? That is what the examples and their description suggest. But if that is so, why does Plato say that there is an overabundance of members of the mixed class (26c8)? He must assume that all things belong to this class that have a well-functioning nature of

---

1. Plato distinguishes the two kinds (the hot and the hotter) in *Politicus* 283a–e, and introduces a separate art of measurement; the fact that he lumps them together here shows that the distinction is irrelevant for his present purposes and that momentary degrees of *apeira* do not constitute a proper mixture.

their own. So not just health and fine weather, but also man and ox would be such mixtures. Their membership in the third class is not immediately obvious, because they are complex entities and contain further successful mixtures, such as physical and mental health and other kinds of good states, as part of their nature. Not only that: Health itself turns out to be a mixture of mixtures (there are many ingredients that have to stand in the right ratio). So there is indeed a great abundance of successful combinations of *peras* and *apeiron*[1].

There is one further point of puzzlement. Why does Plato seem to specify the successful mixture as an equilibrium of *opposites*? It would seem rather odd to define fine weather as the right mixture of frost and heat, or health as the right mixture of fever and hypothermia, not to mention defining the virtue of liberality as the right mixture of stinginess and waste. Was he overly influenced by cases such as music, where the right mixture of high and low sounds happens to be a fitting description? If the idea of such a mixture seems quite wrong for many cases, adjustments are easily made. If we look at the way Plato describes the functioning of the healthy body in the *Timaeus* (69–81e), we see that indeed a combination of hot and cold and a lot of other opposite elements is involved (though not fever and hypothermia). The same may be said for good climate: Plato is not likely to think of permanent sunshine but of the healthy climate that constitutes the yearly weather in the moderate zones, where we have so much rain, so many dry periods, this much warm weather in summer, and that much cold weather in winter. If the right measure prevails, we are spared killing droughts, bitter frost, stifling heat, or deluges. The analogous principle should hold for a virtuous character, embodying the right balance of actions that would otherwise amount to too much or too little.

If Plato has such a carefully orchestrated mixture in mind, it is clear why he mentions *reason* as the only candidate for the fourth class, the class of what causes such a mixture, and why he so emphasizes that it must be identical with the maker, the *demiurge* (27b). In reminding us of the divine demiurge in the *Timaeus* (*Tim.* 29a; 41a), he seems to indicate that only a purposeful design can cause the right balance. Hence only divine and human reason can be designing causes of such mixtures.

After this rough outline of the fourfold division, our next question must be what purpose it serves in the dialogue, and how it is connected with the 'divine method'. Prima facie the connection seems quite superficial,

---

1. That living organisms are harmonious mixtures is the basis of the further discussion of pleasure and pain at 31b ff.

because the concepts of the limit and the unlimited function very differently in the two passages. In the 'divine method', *peras* and *apeiron* were used as *criteria* for the division of the genera as a means to control the numerical completeness of the divisions on every level. In the 'fourfold division', the limit and the unlimited are themselves *genera*. So what affinity is there, apart from the fact that limit and unlimited are in each case connected with 'number' and 'numberlessness'?

I take it that the coherence consists not so much in the quite different application of the same set of terms, but rather in that in the fourfold division Socrates applies the prescriptions of the divine method to the degree that suits his purposes. The application of the method is admittedly quite limited, since division is not carried beyond the separation of the four classes (with bare indications of what subclasses there can be). But Socrates quite pointedly emphasizes the injunction that *generic unity* must be sought and indicates when he omits doing so. Thus he repeatedly calls it their task to 'collect' (*sunagein*) the scattered members of the class under one heading (23e; 25c); he reminds Protarchus that such a reduction under one genus is what the previous argument had enjoined them to produce (25a). He even apologizes for not having established the unity of the 'limit' in the proper fashion (25d).

So there is at least a rudimentary application of the divine method, even if it is not carried out in the way that Socrates had declared necessary for all those who want to be counted as experts in any field. No such expertise is sought here, nor will there be a proper division of all pleasures and intellectual activities later in the dialogue. But the divine method is at least used to establish the unity of the supreme genera of all things in such a way that it allows for pleasure and knowledge to be *subsumed* under one of the four classes. So by the "armament that is partially the same" Plato must refer to the criteria that constitute unity and plurality in the highest genera. Did he regard the fourfold division as complete, as far as the highest level of all things is concerned? This is not the place to test its viability, but the phrase "all there is" seems indeed to suggest that his genera comprise everything.

If, then, there is an inner connection between the divine method and the fourfold division, what place is there for the Forms in that division? The question whether and how the Forms find their place in this schema has exercised past commentators a good deal.[1] But if what has been said about the role of the Forms in the divine method is right, the solution of

1. Cf. Hackforth (1945), 39.

the problem is not difficult to find. If genera and species as depicted in the divine method are Forms (the invariant nature of the entities in question), then the four highest genera of all being must also be Forms, and each of them must contain Forms as their subgenera, species, and subspecies. This is not the generally accepted answer to the question of how the Forms fit in the fourfold division; that it is not must be due to the great heterogeneity of the four classes of being. Few commentators have trouble associating the Forms with the limit. But Forms of the unlimited? Or the mixture? Or its cause? If we leave aside the notion that Plato's Forms are ideal models that we commonly associate with them, but hold on to the fact that the four genera fulfill the injunctions of the divine method, there is no reason why the four highest genera of being should not be Forms, since there are Forms of more specialized kinds of entities. In addition, we should remember the strange Forms recommended in the *Sophist*: the Forms of being, of sameness and difference, and of motion and rest.[1] Plato seems to have no qualms there about accepting highly abstract and formal concepts as kinds of Forms. So there is no good ground for rejecting Forms of the four genera of being, including the Form of the unlimited. Possible consequences for the concept of Form will be discussed later in this essay.

II.4. The genera of pleasure and knowledge (27c–31b).

As Socrates' subsequent procedure shows, the fourfold division of all being is not an excursion into the field of general metaphysics but rather the most important stepping stone towards a definition of pleasure and knowledge, because it allows Socrates to determine the genus they belong to. How important this step is will appear later when their *generic* properties turn out to be the essential criteria for their evaluation.

It comes as no great surprise that the better good, the life that combines pleasure with knowledge, should be a member of the mixed class. Equally unsurprising, pleasure is assigned to the genus of the unlimited; Philebus himself agrees it is essential that pleasure be boundless and ever capable of increase. The classification of knowledge as a member of the fourth class, the *cause* of successful mixtures, is argued for in a much more elaborate fashion. Socrates seems intent on treating the issue in its widest possible perspective. To prove that reason belongs to the genus of cause,

---

1. The subsequent definition of pleasure as a process makes it a close relative of the *Sophist's* Form of motion, which clearly must be of the kind that permits the 'more and less'.

nothing less will do than a comparison between the *macrocosm*, the world
order as a whole in its greatness and splendor, and the *microcosm*, the
human sphere in its smallness, humility, and dependence on the larger
sphere (28a–31a). In both cases a harmonious mixture must have reason
as its cause—divine reason for the world order at large, and human reason
for our affairs.

The argument Socrates uses to prove his point is not only unusually
elaborate; it also provokes angry protests from Philebus and confuses
Protarchus. What angers Philebus is the grandiose way in which Socrates
prepares the definition of his champion, knowledge. Given the preparatory
work in the preceding section, he could easily have shown without further
ado that every successful mixture is the product of reason. If the tiff over
the 'exaltation' of intelligence does not just liven up the discussion, there
must be a further motive for this change in Socrates' style. His elaboration
on the role of reason in the universe hints at a wider perspective for his
fourfold division than the mere need to decide the question of the good
in human life. Most of the time Socrates narrowly confines himself to the
issue at hand, the rivalry between pleasure and knowledge. But occasionally glimpses of further possible consequences of the theory are divulged
here; the consequences concern the order of the universe at large, as well
as its cause.

After division is successfully applied to classify pleasure, knowledge,
and the mixed life, one might expect the discussion soon to be concluded.
The partners have agreed on the mixed life as *the* human good. Pleasure
is an unlimited but somehow necessary ingredient; knowledge is the cause
of all good mixtures, and is therefore also in charge of determining the
right limit of pleasure. From this it would follow that knowledge is indeed
more closely related to the good. Philebus' angry outburst at what he calls
Socrates' "glorification" of his own candidate shows that he is suspicious
of such a drift in the discussion. But Socrates does not go for such an easy
victory. Nor should he, of course, because the result of the fourfold
division does not permit more than a *functional* description of the role of
pleasure and knowledge in the good life. It does not tell us what kinds of
pleasures there should be, nor what kind of limit knowledge must impose
to create a good mixture, nor what kind of knowledge can bring that about.
So there is much more work to be done.

But before we turn to the ensuing detailed discussion of the cause and
ingredients of the good life, we must take up once more the question
why Socrates introduced the complex method of dialectic, the 'gift of the
gods'. For although he made *some* use of its prescriptions, the actual use

is very limited and does not do justice to the method in important respects. Why did Socrates so emphasize the demand that the divisions must be complete and numerically exact, if he did not care to follow this rule himself? And why does he stress that no one who does not follow the rules is ever to count as competent at anything, if he thereby denigrates his own effort?

The most plausible answer is that Plato wanted to make crystal clear what he is *not* doing in the *Philebus*.[1] He wants to leave no doubt that although *some* use is made of the laws of dialectic, his investigation of pleasure and knowledge cannot be called dialectic proper. It is carried only as far as necessary to find the ingredients of the good life. The question about competence is related to this point. By foregoing a system-atic dialectical treatment of all kinds of pleasure and knowledge, the partners forfeit the claim to expertise in those fields. That is to say, Socrates and his partners have become experts neither in the field of pleasure nor in the field of knowledge. The results of the dialogue are therefore, quite intentionally and explicitly, declared by Plato to be limited: The partners get as far as they need to decide their initial question, but no further. So the great fanfare with which Socrates had introduced the divine method is at the same time the indicator of the limitations of his own investigation. "Don't fool yourself," Plato seems to say, "and think that this is dialectic pure and proper." We will get a proper taste of the laboriousness of its real work in the third part of the dialogue, when we follow the limited task of investigating pleasure and knowledge.

III. The "critical" part of the investigation: critique of pleasure and knowledge (31b–59b).

The long middle part of the dialogue, especially the discussion and critique of different kinds of pleasure, is often regarded as somewhat disorganized and overly bogged down in detail. Even when no such judgment is explicit in the secondary literature, the relative neglect of what is, after all, the declared topic of the dialogue speaks for itself.[2] There is, of course, some tedium in working out the details, once the principles are on the table.

---

1. To insist on such a negative purpose for the introduction of the divine method is not to deny that Plato also used it as an opportunity for indicating what the proper method is. Plato often seems to have more than one motive for the way he composed his dialogues.

2. Gosling (1975) devotes 70 pages of his General Commentary to the dialogue's first 20 pages, while 18 pages suffice for the remaining 36 Stephanus pages.

But only the concrete applications show what the principles are worth. In addition, the different points of criticism raised against pleasure and knowledge are not only important for better understanding the principles themselves; they also contain a surprising wealth of information that helps to straighten out what had been left in an unsatisfactory state in previous dialogues. The tedium of the middle part is considerably reduced when those references to Plato's earlier views on pleasure are taken into consideration; we no longer lose the forest for the trees. If anything, then, Plato has somewhat overloaded the discussion in the attempt to clear up those previous records. Although this goal makes the middle part sometimes difficult to follow, it has the virtue that Plato ends up with a coherent theory of pleasure.[1]

It remains to be seen now what benefit is derived from the preceding ontological preparation for the overall treatment of pleasure and knowledge, and in particular to what extent it influences the *critique* of pleasure and knowledge. The fact that pleasure and its counterpart, pain, get much more attention than knowledge shows that the nature of pleasure is the main problem of the dialogue. (Its middle part falls into two sections of very uneven length; pleasure is discussed for more than 20 pages, while four pages suffice for knowledge.) Whether or not it was Plato himself who named the dialogue after the almost silent Philebus and not after his active spokesman Protarchus, the name turns out to be justified, because it is the full spectrum of all pleasures that is here subject to scrutiny. We will have to see why Plato subjects pleasure to such an extensive review and critique.

III.1. The nature of pleasure and pain (31b–36c).

Subsumption of pleasure under the genus of the unlimited provides the basis for precisely determining its nature. Despite their unlimited character, Socrates claims to closely associate pleasure and pain with harmonious mixtures. This does not make them members of that genus themselves. They are rather identified with *processes* of *dissolution* and *restoration*, respectively, in living creatures: "When the natural combination of limit and

---

1. Many issues not settled in earlier dialogues are clarified. What they are will be indicated in notes to the individual passages, to avoid interrupting and overly lengthening this introduction.

unlimitedness that forms a living organism is destroyed, this destruction is pain, while the return towards its own nature, this general restoration, is pleasure" (32b). Besides destruction and restoration there is also a third, neutral, state that might also be feasible for a living creature (32e). Socrates, for reasons of his own, keeps a little under his thumb the fact that this 'also possible' state is actually the mixed state of health and harmony itself, although he gives his partner at least a hint when he expresses the suspicion that it may in fact turn out to be "the most godlike state of all" (33b). He has good reason not to let that cat out of the bag too soon. It would detract from the importance of investigating the different kinds of pleasure if it were obvious right at the beginning that pleasure is at best a *remedial good* and that the state of pleasureless imperturbability is actually preferable. At the end of that long investigation this result will be presented as the most fundamental critical point about pleasure. Pleasure as a process of (re)generation is always only second best in comparison with proper being (53c ff.).

Socrates at first only dimly foreshadows this point, and it is all the easier for Protarchus to miss because of their previous agreement that a life without pleasure is not preferable for a human being (21e). Part of the work of the critical part of the dialogue is to undermine that agreement, or rather to show what its limiting conditions are. But so far a purely neutral state, taken as such, cannot have much attraction in Protarchus' eyes.

The definition of pleasure and pain as *restoration* and *disintegration* may at first baffle rather than enlighten us. Why should such processes be regarded as 'unlimited'? Don't they have a quite definite beginning, middle, and end? Not so, Plato seems to answer, insofar as they are *processes*. What sets limits to them is the nature of the *thing* destroyed and restored, its state of health and harmony which determines the appropriate limit, not the processes of destruction and restoration themselves. Pleasure and pain are therefore not 'self-determined'; what limitations there are to them come from factors other than themselves. Their existence, their duration, and their intensity depend on the causes of the destruction (by frost or heat, for instance) and the kind of harmonious state reached by the restoration (31d–32b). So in and of themselves they are quite unlimited and, although remaining pleasures and pains, always admit a "more and less." Nor do they have an independent existence of their own. Once the organism is restored, both pain and pleasure are gone. This, in a nutshell, is the basic metaphysical account of pleasure and pain of both the body and the soul; it serves as the foundation for the entire subsequent critique, and keeps it focused.[1]

The general definition of pleasure and pain as restoration and destruction, respectively, of a living organism is only the first step in their investigation. Socrates adds various further specifications and qualifications. First he gives a kind of *physiological* account to justify the claim that there is always such a process at work for both body and soul. This physiological explanation at the same time clarifies in what sense the distinction between pleasures of the *body* and pleasures of the *soul* is to be understood. There are, strictly speaking, no pleasures or pains of the body alone; the soul must at least take notice of the respective processes of destruction and restoration in the body. Under 'pleasures or pains of the soul' we are to understand from now on only those in which the body is not involved. As an example, Socrates refers to the pleasure of expectation: We sometimes enjoy a future replenishment before it actually takes place. Such pleasant anticipations happen without an actual process in the body.

Further considerations show that it is not correct to equate even the simple pains and pleasures of hunger and eating only with emptying and refilling the organism. *Memory* and *desire* turn out to play an important role in these processes as well. Hunger is not the plain feeling of emptiness; only a newborn baby has that sheer pain. For *us*, who possess memory of previous experiences of this kind, hunger always already contains the desire for the corresponding replenishment that we remember. So there are complex feelings of the longing soul connected with the sheer pain of the body in need.

What is the use of all this refinement? It explains, first of all, how complex our simple-looking so-called physical pleasures and pains actually are. (It will emerge later that most pleasures and pains are actually mixed phenomena, a fact that will turn out to have important consequences for Plato's analysis of the emotions in 47d–50e.) It also explains that the soul plays a considerable role in all of them. For it is the soul's business to know the object of the pleasure in question and to procure it. Thus the soul is responsible for determining a pleasure's 'intentional object', what the pleasure is *about* (35b). This analysis of the complexity of pleasure and pain provides the basis for discovering the promised *discrimination* among different kinds of pleasures and identifying their different kinds of *flaws*.

---

1. For a fuller discussion of the issue, cf. D. Frede (1992).

For if pleasures are always defined by their content, their intentional object, we can be mistaken about them in various ways. Therefore pleasures can be false.

III.2. The question of 'false pleasures' (36c–50e).

The question whether Socrates is justified in his distinction between 'true and false pleasures' has stirred up a lot of discussion.[1] Indeed an abundance of different kinds of 'falsenesses' is distinguished here, and commentators who accuse Plato of *equivocation* in the use of true and false are justified. In his exoneration it must be said that he does not hide the equivocation, but is quite explicit about it when he announces more and more 'falsities'. He takes them on, one by one, and explains quite clearly what each falsity or wrongness consists in. So there is no cheating here; Socrates merely exploits the manifold colloquial uses of 'false'. Because he has to develop the criteria for judging pleasures along with the explanation of the origin of those pleasures, the discussion is too complex to unravel here all its details. It seems better first to give a kind of catalogue of the different types of flaws, and then to add some comments on the rationale for the distinctions.

(1) There are false pleasures and pains in the *literal* sense of truth and falsity (36c–41a). Pleasures are here taken to have a propositional content,[2] so what is falsely enjoyed is an assumed fact or state of affairs as defined by its *description*.

(2) Pleasures and pains can be false in the sense that they are *overrated* in size and worth. In this case a 'false amount' of pleasure is enjoyed or pain endured. This means that the amount exceeding the measure that is truly warranted has to be regarded as false (41a–42c).

1. An analysis of pleasures as attitudes involving beliefs was first suggested by Bernard Williams, "Pleasure and Belief," *Proceedings of the Aristotelian Society*, Supplementary Vol. 1959, 57–72. On false pleasures cf. the Gosling-Kenny debate; Gosling (1959), (1961), Kenny (1960), continued by, among others, Dybikowsky (1970), Penner (1970), and myself (1985).

2. Pleasure is a 'propositional attitude' if not 'things' are enjoyed, such as an apple or a glass of wine, but presumed states of affairs. Snow White's evil stepmother, e.g., enjoys not her own beauty but the alleged fact 'that she is the fairest of all'. The content of the pleasure consists in a statement or 'proposition', as philosophers prefer to call it.

(3) Pleasure is false when it is confused with the neutral state of painlessness. Here the falsity concerns the assumption of what pleasure itself *is* (42c–44b).

(4) There is falsity in the kinds of pleasures that are *intrinsically* mixed with pain. Here falsity concerns the *impurity* of pleasure. Such falseness (= impurity) exists in so-called pleasures of the body (44c–47d), in pleasures of the soul and body, and in pleasures of the soul alone (47d–50d).

The discussion of these four kinds of 'falsity' is followed by a brief discussion of the true pleasures (51a–53c), and the whole part is concluded by a general criticism of pleasure as a good from a purely ontological point of view. Pleasure, it is pointed out, is always a process of *becoming* and must by its very nature be regarded as a good inferior to whatever has solid *being* (53c–55c). But before we can turn to this conclusion and its consequences, we need to comment further on the different types of falsity.

(1) The first type of 'falsity', i.e., falsity in the literal sense, has given rise to strong objections, both against Socrates from his partner Protarchus' side and against Plato from the side of modern critics who do not accept his conception of 'propositional pleasures' of the kind characterized here as 'false enjoyment of alleged facts or states of affairs'. Protarchus is unusually tenacious in his opposition. (After his initial recalcitrance against the distinction among pleasures at the very beginning of the dialogue, this is the only point at which he resists.) His resistance has one obvious effect: It gives Socrates the opportunity for an unusually thorough investigation. There is a gradual buildup towards establishing false propositional pleasures, with several setbacks on the way. At first Socrates argues only for an *analogy* between true judgments and true pleasures. Is there not a parallel, in the sense that both may be mistaken about their *object*, while there is, in each case, a real judgment and a real pleasure? Once this is granted, Socrates can inch his way closer to his goal. He does so by a fairly elaborate description of how the soul arrives at its beliefs, especially its long-term beliefs about the world, and he supplements this by depicting a painter in the soul who provides illustrations of those *logoi*. Now many of these *logoi* and painted *phantasmata* concern the future and are called hopes. And many such hopes will turn out to be false. Such pleasant anticipations must be considered false pleasures, and the corresponding fears false pains. This, in short, is Socrates' argument which, after some haggling about detail, in the end wins his partner's consent.

Should it have done so? If everything is, logically speaking, above board, why did Socrates not explain in a more direct way that some pleasures consist in *logoi* or *pictures*? It would seem that his reasons are mainly psychological; had he taken such a direct route, Protarchus would not have understood him, as we can see from the fact that even after the long argument he is not quite sure how, precisely, the conclusion was obtained and what it entails (cf. 41a). Should we ourselves, who are more used to such philosophical monsters as 'propositional attitudes', agree to the argument's presuppositions? Does it make sense to call some *logoi* pleasures? Are not feelings one thing and propositions another? This seems to be exactly the point on which Plato disagrees. Socrates' analysis makes clear that pleasures for him are defined by their object, so there is never just pleasure, pure and simple, but always 'the pleasure *in* x, y, or z'. We might, of course, reject this conception of pleasure and take up the cudgel, once again, for Protarchus' initial tenet that pleasures are mere feelings, separable from their occasion and devoid of content; but that position has been disputed by Socrates, so at this juncture an intrinsic relationship between each pleasure and its intentional object is assumed. If we agree to this basic conception, there is no further point in contesting false propositional pleasures where the objects consist in assumed states of affairs.

The more refined among Plato's critics take on a different problem. They hold that what is enjoyable in false anticipatory pleasures is at best the entertainment of a thought, the mental event, while only the thought itself is true. But once again it is questionable whether we are really entitled to drive a wedge between this kind of pleasure and the thought it consists in. Merely *entertaining* the thought that I will win in the lottery is not what is pleasant, if by entertaining we mean 'basking in it'; anticipating the presumed fact itself is what is pleasant. 'Enjoying falsely' is no further removed from the content of the pleasure than 'thinking falsely' or 'saying falsely' is removed from its intentional content.[1] To do justice to Plato's position we will have to accept his supposition that some thoughts are pleasant, some painful, and some emotionally neutral.[2]

---

1. Cf. the critique in Gosling's commentary (1975), 314 ff.; for a discussion of the ample literature and a defense of Plato's analysis against his critics, see D. Frede (1986), 165 ff.

2. Not all pleasures are pleasures of thought; immediate physical pleasures do not presuppose a propositional content. Nor are all pleasures related to thoughts true or false, but only those that enjoy something *as a fact*. Plato's hopes are true or false only if they imply a commitment that something is going to be the case ("I will be rich").

Once we get used to treating some pleasures as thoughts or pictures, there still remains the question why Socrates concentrated so much on false hopes. This focus has misled many of Plato's critics, because it gave rise to the debate whether just the pictur*ing* of the pleasure is enjoyed, rather than the picture. Picturing may be pleasant or unpleasant, the objection to Plato runs, but it can be true or false only in a derivative sense. That Plato is not concerned with picturing as such becomes clear if we take seriously Socrates' assertion that the same account of false pleasures applies to cases in the present and in the past (40d). I can enjoy false representations of both present and past, and it is clear that such enjoyment is not a matter of picturing or daydreaming. Further, it is easy to explain why Socrates focused on the future rather than on the present or past. It would have been much harder to convince his partner that what is enjoyed in the present is not the *thing* itself, but rather the thing *as conceived of* by the person. It would be easier for past than for present pleasures to argue that they must consist in thoughts and pictures, because the events themselves are no longer there to be enjoyed. I may, for instance, entertain false pleasures about past successes or false pains about alleged failures. But it would take detailed argument and subtle psychological analysis to show in what sense they can be false. The matter is much simpler when we are concerned with pleasant anticipations of the future, for anticipated facts clearly do not yet exist; in fact, they often turn out to be blatantly and crushingly false. Clearly all there is to future pleasures are the *logoi* or pictures in the soul, as in the case of the famous dairymaid's pleasant calculations.

The importance of justifying 'propositional pleasures' goes beyond the trite point that we can be mistaken about the alleged facts we enjoy. Once it is clear that the *content* of a pleasure is up for judgment, we need not confine our analysis to questions of factual truth. There is also the possibility of a moral evaluation of pleasures. Plato gives some indication in that direction when he compares the fool's pleasures, which are often false, with those of the good man, beloved by the gods, which are usually true; but he does not comment on the question at this point. The importance of this consideration will resurface in his critique of the emotions (47d ff.).

(2) In the case of the second type of false pleasures, falsity is taken to mean that the size of pleasure and pain are misjudged. Such pleasures are false because they are *inflated* (41b–42c). Plato had already exploited the notion that pleasures and pains have a *size* in the *Protagoras* where somewhat perversely, he lets Socrates defend the thesis that virtue is nothing

but the art of measuring pleasure and pain (*Prt.* 356a–357b). Whether Plato was serious in propounding that theory is debatable. That he brings up the possibility of miscalculating the size of pleasures in the much later *Philebus* shows that he at least still finds such a "hedonic calculus" intriguing. Seen close up, pleasures may appear enormous, so that they diminish our estimate of any subsequent pain. What is false about such a pleasure? Plato expresses himself as if we are enjoying a false portion, in the sense that we might cut off the inflated part and truly enjoy the fraction that is actually warranted. This is no doubt to be taken in a figurative way. Be that as it may, clearly the argument again depends on Plato's assumption that pleasures have a propositional content. No such falsity of inflated pleasures and pains would be conceivable if they were not enjoyed or endured *as* having a certain size and price. It is a matter of rational calculus to find out whether or not the projected pleasure or pain is inflated.

(3) The pleasures that are so false as to be *no pleasures* at all present a more serious problem (42c–44d). At first Plato might seem just to be discarding another so-called falsity familiar to us from everyday life: We call things 'false' that are not at all what they are supposed to be, such as false friends who are no friends, or a false pregnancy which is no pregnancy. But Plato is not concerned with collecting as many colloquial senses of 'false' as possible. Nor is he concerned mainly with the psychological fact that when we are in great distress, we might be tempted to call a state of freedom from pain 'pleasure'. He includes this kind of 'even falser pleasure' because it represents an important theoretical error about its nature: To call a state of undisturbance 'pleasure' clearly violates Plato's definition of pleasure as the *restoration* of a disturbance.

Plato has made the point before that there is a neutral state besides pleasure and pain. Why does he repeat it here? I mentioned earlier that Socrates has kept rather quiet about the fact that the seemingly unattractive neutral state is identical with the highly desirable undisturbed harmonious mixture, although he uttered the suspicion that it might be the "most godlike" of all (33b). Now he has the opportunity to add further specifications. First, he points out that the neutral state is, at least in principle, not incompatible with the assumption that human beings are in constant flux. Only some of the constant changes in us are intense enough to be noticeable and to cause pleasure and pain; so even if the flux theory holds, we are not condemned to oscillate constantly between pleasure and pain. But the feasibility of a life of tranquillity is clearly not his point here; his concern is to defeat a theorist whose highest aim is a state of tranquillity but who insists on calling it pleasure. To draw a sharp line between his own position and that of this antihedonist who has donned a hedonist's hat by calling absense of pain pleasure must be of great importance for Plato, if he wants to insure that his own position is properly understood. The antihedonist is called the "true enemy of Philebus" (44b6) because he would do away altogether with pleasure as Philebus understands it.

Did such a person exist? This question has intrigued commentators, because the detailed information about his personality ("tremendous reputation in natural science," "a harsh nature but not without nobility") and his psychological motivation ("inordinate hatred of pleasure," "regards its attractiveness as witchcraft," 44b–c) suggests that Plato has a definite person and not a dummy in mind. The very fact that Plato blames psychological reasons rather than a proper theory for his attitude (44c6) makes it plausible that he expects his audience to know to whom he is referring. Unfortunately all attempts to identify this killjoy have been unsuccessful, because the theory attributed to him does not jibe well with the known theory of any of the candidates suggested.[1]

Fortunately our ignorance in that respect does not affect our understanding of Plato's point. He not only introduces this curmudgeon to mark out his own position more clearly; he also follows up this man's psychological motivation and explains what causes such fundamental prejudice against pleasure. The prejudice arises because it is very tempting to study pleasure in its most extreme form, and in those cases an inherent flaw is always at work. So although the enemy of Phileban pleasures is mistaken in his views on pleasure because he takes the most extreme case as typical, his antipathy makes him a useful guide to uncovering yet another of pleasure's faults, the fault of being inextricably mixed with pain.

(4) The treatment of 'false', in the sense of *impure* or *mixed*, pleasures takes even more space than Socrates needed for his original defense of false pleasures (44e–50e). They receive this extensive treatment because, first, they represent a type of falsity that is actually shared by the majority of pleasures. For if all pleasures are based on restoring some preceding

1. M. Schofield pleads for Speusippus (1971), but does not manage to overcome the discrepancies between Plato's harsh antihedonists and other reports on Speusippus' position. K. Bringmann (1972) argues with more plausibility for Heracleides Ponticus; the evidence is rather slim, and it is hard to see that the 'pompousness' his contemporaries satirized is the harshness of Plato's man. Since Plato as a younger man held strong antihedonist views (as witnessed in the *Phaedo*) he might be giving a humorous reference to his former self, but it is unlikely that he would have called himself "a powerful scientist" (44b9).

disturbance or lack and if most deficient states are painful in some sense, then most pleasures must inevitably involve pain.[1] The pleasure of assuaging one's hunger is not only preceded by a state of pain, it also lasts only as long as there is pain: Once the hunger is gone, the pleasure of eating is gone too. But here Plato is concerned not so much with these relatively harmless pleasures, as with the extreme types that not only involve pain but are actually *intensified* by pain. We may call them 'morbid pleasures'. His claim is, and he documents it with a kind of medical account, that in morbid states we are more excitable than normally because such states produce a more-than-natural craving. So pleasures of excess are based on a vicious state of body and/or soul. Socrates is primarily addressing sexual indulgence (in a rare flare-up of normally quite subdued humor) and discusses in great detail the bittersweetness of the Phileban erotic pleasures that know no bounds. His insistence on the morbidity of such pleasures gives him the most persuasive argument against a life of pleasure. Who in his senses would prefer a life of constant unhealthy agitation? We should take note here that Plato is not appealing to our moral or aesthetic sense (although his rhetorical flourish is quite remarkable); rather, he is treating the question almost from a *medical* point of view. Such pleasures are the pleasures of someone who suffers from inflammation and are therefore to be avoided.

The morbid pleasures are not confined to the body but include the emotions of the *soul* as well (47d ff.). If we expect Plato to denounce the emotions once again as a kind of black horse that drags us into vice and robs reason of its control (cf. *Phaedr.* 253c–254e), we will find ourselves pleasantly disappointed. He does not fasten on the thesis, as he has done so often before, that emotions represent a conflict between the three parts of the soul (no tri-partition is ever mentioned). His diagnosis is innovative and much subtler than the earlier treatments: He points up a tension within the emotions themselves. All our emotive states, such as wrath, fear, longing, mourning, love, jealousy, or envy, contain a portion of their opposite. As a witness, he calls on Homer's description of the bittersweetness of wrath. What precisely does he have in mind? I take it he does not so much mean the kind of therapeutic delight we might take in storming around; he means that rage itself already implies the sweetness of anticipated revenge. So rage is not a state of unmitigated pain, it is a *mixed state* that already contains a certain amount of pleasure. We can see

1. Even a mild feeling of need would count as a pain. 'Pain' is here the collective term for all *negative* states, including any kind of discomfort, dislike, boredom, or irritation.

now why, in his earlier account of pleasure and pain, he so carefully worked out the function of desire and memory (34c–35d). If desire and memory always to some degree import the opposite of the present state, then each emotion is an amalgam of pleasure and pain.

This principle Plato applies to all our emotive states, both positive and negative. The upshot is that all our emotions have an 'edge' in them, both the soul's sorrows (there is joy in tragedy) and its delights (there is still pain in the pleasure of restoration). To justify his diagnosis, he chooses the example of comic laughter (48a). Comic amusement would seem at first quite unsuitable for this purpose, because it is usually regarded as among the most innocent of all pleasant emotions. What pain could be involved in it? Plato regards the very fact that we laugh when our neighbors or friends make fools of themselves as a sign that we bear them some secret ill will. If this were not so, we would not laugh at their misfortunes but would be genuinely sorry for them. Therefore such laughter pre-supposes at least some kind of inherent malice, a negative, i.e., painful, state of the soul.

Is this analysis of comic amusement plausible? We should grant Plato at least this much: In comic scenes, both on stage and in real life, we do laugh at follies that others commit out of ignorance, and yet would not at all be amused to be in that condition ourselves. (Comic self-laughter was not part of ancient comedy and may be an acquired taste in our culture, if we are capable of it at all.) Why would we like to watch such scenes, if we did not harbor some resentment against others, a *need* to see them make fools of themselves? Such a need is a kind of pain (if all negative states fall under that category), so Plato can claim that the amusement arises out of an impure emotional state: It compensates for some emotional need. Plato's position gains in plausibility when we look at the two cases he is contrasting here. We are amused at someone else's coming to harm only as long as the person is harmless and cannot 'take it out on us'. If such a person is powerful, we are not amused but are afraid of the person's rage. So in the first case it cannot be the intrinsic funniness that makes us laugh, but our estimation that we can give free reign to our *Schadenfreude* in seeing a person come to harm, whereas in the case of the powerful person we think only of the coming explosion.

Whether or not we fully agree with Plato's diagnosis of what constitutes comic amusement we should reflect on the kind of *need* or *irritation* that underlies all our emotions. This may well account for the edge we experience in most such cases. Pure emotions seem to be rare indeed (or nonexistent if Plato is right). Plato does not deny that it is 'only human' to laugh and to weep, or to laugh-and-weep, but he obviously wants to find out why it is human to do so.

This critique of our enjoyment of tragedy and comedy is much subtler than the more famous argument against the arts in the *Republic*. For now Plato is not concerned with the seductiveness of mimicry, nor with the turmoil and error that may be caused by the arts, but simply with the diagnosis of the inner state that makes such pleasures attractive. Nor does Plato say that we would be better off without them. His diagnosis leaves open the question whether we can do without them or whether the emotions created by the arts might not on occasion be quite therapeutic, provided they do not lead to more unhealthy excitement in the soul of theater fanatics. If he takes human beings' emotional make-up to be always in some state of need or other, Plato may have anticipated to some degree the cathartic effect of the tragic and comic emotions that Aristotle was later to discuss. Unfortunately Plato's discussion remains too sketchy to permit a clear decision on this issue.

III.3. True pleasures (50e–55b).

The long disquisition on the different types of falsity of pleasure is a preparation for the *true* pleasures that do not share the flaws previously discussed. The principle of selection works cumulatively. Only those pleasures are acceptable that pass all tests, and those are very few indeed (51a ff.). But not only must the pleasures themselves be factually true, of the right size, and unmixed with pain; the objects of our pleasures must also be pure, stable, and free of limiting conditions. Pleasures of the senses pass the test only when their objects are pure and when the condition of the restoration is only an *unfelt lack*.[1] Such are the delights we take in the impressions of pure white or in pure sounds, pure geometrical shapes, and to a lesser degree, beautiful smells. There is also the pleasure of learning, which does not presuppose a 'felt lack' because its loss and the state of not knowing are not actually painful. This kind of pleasure is reserved for the chosen few with a natural affinity to learning.

This is at first sight a disappointingly austere program, more restrictive than seems warranted by the previous enumeration of 'falsities'. Why

---

1. It is important to see that Plato assumes a lack even for these pleasures. It shows that he regards a general deficiency of human nature as the basis for pleasure throughout, even though he is not nearly as explicit about our intrinsic neediness as he is in the *Symposium* (200a ff.)

should Plato want to confine us to the scanty enjoyment of such things as pure patches of white, of pure sounds, or perfectly straight lines while banishing such innocent pleasures as those we may take in inspecting a whole picture or in listening to a melody? His claim that in all these cases the objects' beauty is relative to the context seems rather implausible. Where does this relativity condition come from all of a sudden? We may grant him that the most beautiful colors in the wrong combination look ugly, just as the most beautiful sounds may make a discord. But not all beautiful sounds in melodies or beautiful colors in paintings do that. So why not allow for more complex pieces of art? Is this just a new manifestation of the old Platonic 'ontological prejudice' that whatever allows for variety is inferior to what does not?

There may be prejudice here, but it is not just the prejudice against variability and relativity. When Plato now separates the pure and unadulterated from the violent, multiform, and quantitatively enormous (52c) and makes the former pleasures honorary members of the 'limited' class, this discrimination against the multiform must be based on the morbidity claim that he made for all violent pleasures. They all depend on a *contrast*, on an inner tension that is capable of unlimited increase. So here he is cashing in on that claim and insinuating that pleasures in sounds, colors, and shapes are genuine only if they owe nothing to any such contrast but are enjoyed in and of themselves. If the beauty of a composition gives pleasure because it combines contrasting elements, it does so because it creates a sensual and intellectual excitement that stirs up the need for further increase and continued variety in such entertainment.

This concern for purity in pleasure may strike us as rather puritanical. But such purism becomes more palatable, at least from a philosophical point of view, if we keep in mind the agreement that the perfect life is the life without needs. If that life is not attainable, limitation of need is the next best state. Plato is simply adhering to this tenet when he recommends only limited pleasures: When we get our 'fill' of pure white and enjoy it, it makes no difference whether we see a small patch or a large one, whether we see it for a short time or longer. The multiform pleasures that depend on contrast and variation stimulate our appetite for more and more, because the pleasures' objects are not purely and simply what they are; our feelings are ambiguous. Multiform pleasures create restlessness and excite our curiosity to look for ever new and different impressions.[1] That Plato was no friend of cultural innovations is nothing new to us; the

---

1. Cf. the *Timaeus'* account of the contrast between different kinds of sound (80a–b).

narrow limit he sets for true pleasures seems based on his old concern that disturbances should be kept away from the soul, although he is silent here about their social consequences. These psychological explanations are not likely to reconcile us to Plato's austerity program, but at least they enlighten us about a fundamental fact of human nature: Our need for cultural innovations is always a state of *need*, so the pleasures we derive from them are bought at a price. It is the price of eternal restlessness and discontent.

Once the simple, true, and pure pleasures are selected, Plato turns to a general criticism of the nature of pleasure from a purely *ontological* point of view (53c ff.). All pleasures have in common one feature, that rules out the possibility that any of them can be an unqualified good, namely, that pleasure by its very nature is always a *becoming (aei genesis estin)* and has no *being (ousia)*. This quite general critique should come as no surprise. It merely sums up what is implied in the definition of pleasure as a process of restoration, if restoration can be called a kind of becoming, too. If the word '*genesis*' had not previously been used, then the expression "return to its own nature" comes close enough (32b3: *hodos eis ten hauton ousian*).[1] But only now does Socrates make explicit that this is his most important reservation concerning pleasure. He refers to authority here as well, some "subtle thinkers" to whom they owe "quite some gratitude" for this insight (53c). There can be little doubt that this is Plato's own doctrine, and it is a doctrine that he has ascribed in a slightly different form to a very subtle thinker elsewhere. The wise Diotima in her lecture on love had already enlightened Socrates on man's eternal vacillation; human beings are depicted in the *Symposium* as needy creatures in a state of eternal becoming because of their constant need of fulfillment and regeneration (cf. *Symp.* 201d ff., esp. 207d).[2]

Here the emphasis is not so much on a constant need for self-restoration, but rather on the fundamental distinction between two kinds of states: those that are never more than processes of becoming, a means to a further end; and those that have a stable being and are a self-sufficient

---

1. In the fourfold division, the creation of a harmonious mixed state is called a *genesis eis ousian*; so the distinction between being and becoming lurks in the background of the critique of pleasure from the very beginning.

2. In the *Philebus*, the reference to the lover and the loved (53c–d) as an illustration of the relationship between being and becoming bewilders rather than enlightens Protarchus; it must be meant as a pointer to the *Symposium*, where the relation between lover and the beloved is, quite naturally, Diotima's paradigm.

end in themselves. Pleasure is therefore always just a process of regeneration, and persons who choose it as their life-style condemn themselves
to an inferior life. Not only that, they also condemn themselves to a
life of constant destruction, because all regeneration is preceded by
destruction, so the pleasure-lovers live a seesaw life (54d–55a). As Socrates and Protarchus now agree, it is a life quite inferior to the neutral third
type of life, one spent in pure thought. So even at its very best, pleasure
is only a remedial good. Its goodness depends entirely on the end attained
by the process of regeneration.

This claim may seem questionable, since Socrates does not explicitly
include here the pure pleasures which he had previously made honorary
members of the limited class. But since even the 'intake' of pure objects
of the senses or of learning presupposes a *lack*, albeit a painless one, even
pure and true pleasures are only "fillings," *viz*. processes of becoming. As
processes they possess only a vicarious goodness, since the end attained
is superior to the process that leads up to it. Knowing is better than
learning.

This concludes Plato's treatment of pleasure as a relative good. Its
classification as a remedial good in the *Philebus* permits him to leave out
all (or nearly all) polemical arguments of the type familiar from Plato's
earlier work. Pleasure as such is no longer an ontologically suspect phenomenon; if it is not to be cultivated for its own sake, it is because that
would mean the cultivation of incompleteness. The remedial pleasures
that compensate the unavoidable destructions of living organisms must
be welcome for restoration's sake only, as must be the pleasures of
learning, because they compensate for our state of original ignorance.
People who choose a life of pleasure for its own sake condemn themselves
to Sisyphean labors, to creating ever new needs to have something to
fulfill. So sybarites will find themselves in strange company.[1]

The result of this 'ontological critique' concerns not only the firm
entrenchment of pleasure on the side of becoming. Other important
corollaries are to be considered as well. If pleasure as becoming is in the
genus of the unlimited, are all other members of that class processes as
well? We have little evidence to decide this question, but if it were so we
would understand why Plato addressed the members of that class as "the
hotter" and "the colder," the faster and the slower, etc. We would also

---

1. Plato has therefore not given up the view professed in the *Gorgias* that pleasure hunting
is a Sisyphean labor (493b–494b). However, he has given up the view that man can live a
life without needs.

understand why he displays such insouciance when he groups together without compunction the hot, the hotter, the too hot, heat-waves, and fever. Items in the unlimited class are not tied down by any definite measure, so they are liable to constant change, even if they are not always actually in flux. So the Heraclitean Flux remains, but it is corralled in *one* specific genus, the genus of the unlimited.[1]

Another consequence of this ontological division is that Plato can now attribute definite *being* to some sensible objects. For all those items that belong to the mixed class will have *being*; they possess a definite and harmonious nature as long as they are in that state. Not just health, strength, and beauty, but *our* health, our strength, our beauty will possess a definite nature. The equilibrium in each case may be instable, since it depends on material conditions, but as long as it lasts we can say with precision what that thing or quality is.[2] This seems to represent a considerable change of mind in Plato, because it allows him to make distinctions between the ontological status of different kinds of sensible objects. He may of course already have assumed such a distinction among sensibles in earlier dialogues, but if so, he only now provides the precise ontological categories for doing so, with the help of the four genera of being.[3]

Are the benefits of the 'divine method' confined to establishing the generic unity of pleasure as a member of the unlimited class? Since it has sometimes been suggested in the literature that Plato actually applies 'division' in the long discussion of false pleasures, the question of the divine method's methodological payoff should be taken up briefly. Socrates does separate the pleasures of the soul from the pleasures of the body. But that division is not carried any further. The distinction between true and false pleasures is not a proper division, because pleasures of the same sort may be true in certain circumstances and false in others. Not all our dairymaid-like pleasures are necessarily false; nor do we necessarily share

1. This explains his generous hand waving to the flux theorists at 43a–b.

2. This theory more than accidentally resembles the structure which the Demiurge imposes on material entities to end the flux in the *Timaeus*. The dialogues differ insofar as the "limit" of the *Philebus* is replaced by atomic structure in the *Timaeus*.

3. This takes care of Waterfield's (1980) and Hampton's (1990) contention that there is no difference of any importance between the *Republic* and the *Philebus*. True, the *Philebus* keeps *being* and *becoming* as separate as ever, but there are now some *gignomena* that actually achieve *ousia*, and others that cannot do so by definition. It may be a sound maxim that a phrase like "*genesis eis ousian*" or "*gegenemene ousia*" should not be overinterpreted, as Hackforth says (49n2). But they should also not be underinterpreted, especially not when they are based on a proper theory.

Esau's predicament in wrongly assessing the size and worth of our pleasures and pains. Even the dichotomy between pure and impure pleasures
does not fulfill the criteria for division, since the limiting conditions must
be used in a cumulative manner to sort out the acceptable kinds from the
unacceptable ones (true, pure, unmixed . . .).

That Plato does not carry out a full-scale division is not due only to
the unsuitability of truth and falsehood as criteria of classification. The
definition of pleasure as a process of restoration or the filling of a lack
indicates why performing such a division might be a hopeless task, quite
generally. There is an enormous range of possible disturbances and restorations of the harmonious equilibrium of both body and soul. As Plato
says in the *Republic* (445c), there is only one state of perfection, but there
are infinitely many states of deficiency. In the *Republic* he selected and
discussed four, just as he selects specific kinds of incompletenesses in the
Philebus, but he can clearly enumerate no more than a few. To aim
at completion would mean to classify all lacks and diseases and their
restorations. This probably explains why Socrates resorted to his 'sudden
memory' at 20b and avoided the task of displaying his expertise in dialectic.

What, then, did Plato achieve in his long investigation of pleasure, and
what were his criteria of selection? He clearly fulfilled his promise to sort
out different types of pleasures according to the criteria that were discussed
in connection with Socrates' dream. The good must be *complete, sufficient,*
and *desirable* for all. In the section on false pleasures, Plato pointed out
in how many ways and for what reasons different pleasures may fall short
of those conditions. As processes of regeneration, so Socrates has shown,
pleasures are neither complete in themselves nor sufficient, and even the
best of them are desirable only on the condition that they lead to a
state of harmony. This interpretation will be corroborated later with the
selection of the ingredients of a perfect human life (59d–64b).

III.4. The critique of knowledge: its pure and impure forms (55c–59b).

In the case of knowledge, possible flaws obviously cannot amount to
falsehood, since 'false knowledge' is not knowledge at all. The criterion
of truth is therefore applied in the sense of *purity*, and it becomes clear
now why Plato emphasized it so much in his critique of pleasure: If the
two rivals are to be compared, there must be a sufficient common basis.
Plato's testing of knowledge proceeds, once again, on the basis of a
rudimentary division of all intellectual activities. But the division is not

carried beyond the preliminary distinction between the productive arts and crafts on the one side, and the 'educational' disciplines of the liberal arts on the other. The criterion used to test the purity of the different kinds of knowledge obviously does not establish further subdivisions, for it cuts across all the arts and sciences: In all disciplines it is the degree of mathematical accuracy that determines the level of purity. In each art, removing its mathematical elements (that allow for counting, measuring, weighing, and the requisite instruments) would leave only routine, practice, and experience by trial and error. Is this really a fair criterion for evaluating the desirability of different disciplines for the good life? Or is it just a manifestation of yet another prejudice, namely, Plato's preoccupation with mathematics?

We should reflect on the reasons for Plato's preoccupation with mathematics as the main clue to reality. He believed that if knowledge is to be stable and reliable, routine and experience are insufficient. Real knowledge must be of the stable structures behind the appearances. And such knowledge can be had only if we understand the mathematically determined relations that constitute such structures. That Plato entertained the hope that mathematics will provide us with such knowledge is nothing new; his optimism in that regard explains the decisive role that mathematics plays in his educational program in the seventh book of the *Republic* (522c–531c). His insistence on purity for the different kinds of intellectual disciplines in terms of *accuracy* in the *Philebus* seems a conscious reminder of that doctrine. For here, too, Plato points out the inferiority of the purely empirical aspect of the applied sciences, and even the catalogue of disciplines is almost the same: Music, agriculture, navigation, and strategy are on both lists, and in both cases he stresses the need to keep the mathematical sciences themselves free of empirical elements. If there is any difference, it lies in the *Philebus'* explicit demand for a strict dichotomy between pure ("philosophical") and applied sciences (building and trading arts, 56d–57e), so actually two quite different disciplines clearly share the name of mathematics. And in both dialogues *dialectic* is assigned a place above all other sciences. It alone is not concerned with the changeable objects of this world, the objects of belief (*doxa*, 58e–59b), as are so many of the so-called sciences. Once again, the Forms are the objects of dialectic, as the examples make quite clear. For although the objects of 'real knowledge' are not called "Forms," it is difficult to see what else Plato might be addressing as "the things that are forever in the same state, without anything mixed in it" (59c), things that have "true reality" (59d). The objects of exact science mentioned a little later are "justice itself" and "the circle and the divine sphere itself" (62a). So in the *Philebus* a two-world theory is asserted once again.

This reassertion of a two-world point of view and of the contrast between the Forms and perishables provides a much treasured resource for all those who claim that Plato never changed his mind about the Forms. But to the reader of the *Philebus* itself it must come as something of a surprise. Plato's earlier treatment of the divine method suggests that it does not much matter whether or not the objects of a science are treated as Forms, as long as the injunctions concerning the *limit* and the *unlimited* are conscientiously observed. Are there two notions of dialectic in our dialogue, one that concerns method only, and another that specializes in the unchangeable ideal objects? Such a 'splitting' of the art of dialectic cannot be a satisfactory solution, because the dialectical method had been introduced to solve the "real problem of the One and Many" that Plato characterized as a problem about the Forms (15a–b). Perhaps we were mistaken, then, in assuming that the divine method could be applied to all sciences, and perhaps Plato now wants to draw our attention to the fact that, properly speaking, the divine method is applicable only if the objects of the various disciplines are eternal, ideal, and invariable Forms?[1] In this case Socrates' elucidation of the method was highly misleading; neither the letters of the alphabet nor the sounds and rhythms of music were treated as if they represent Forms that exist in strict separation from their sensible instances. Nor is such a split easily reconciled with the fourfold division of all being. If the class of the unlimited forms a true *genus* of what there is, how can its members, the hotter and colder, etc., be understood as Forms? But if the fourfold division has no room in Plato's metaphysical theory, as it is presented now, why did he go into the lengthy macrocosm-microcosm argument to establish divine reason as the supreme cause of successful mixtures of limit and the unlimited?[2] And why did he introduce the problem of 'the one and many' as if it did relate to the problem of the plurality of pleasures? This was, after all, his motive for subsuming pleasure under the genus of the unlimited and for submitting it to a systematic critique. A closer look at the special mixture of the good life will, perhaps, help us weave together the disparate strands of Plato's argument.

1. On the problem of the Forms in the *Philebus*, cf. Fahrnkopf (1977), Shiner (1979), Mohr (1983), and Shiner's Response (1983); Sayre (1983), ch. 3.

2. Since the harmonious order of the soul is mentioned as a harmonious mixture (26b), justice itself must be the Form of such a mixture.

IV. The "synthetic" part of the discussion: mixing together the good life (59b–64b).

In the final mixture a kind of pragmatism seems to prevail over purism. A life of knowledge alone is declared not choiceworthy for a human being; and even in a mixed life more than the best type of knowledge is needed if the right mixture is to do justice to the peculiar situation of human beings and to fulfill their practical needs. The superhuman knowledge of ideal entities would not help us deal with the tasks of everyday life. So the 'best life' mixture is to contain both pure and impure forms of knowledge. All arts and sciences are necessary, so Plato admits even those that are, like music, full of "lucky hits and imitation" (62c). For practical purposes, we need the applied sciences not in spite of, but because of, their impreci-sion. With this compromise, does Plato renounce his insistence on the purity of the sciences that is so forcefully documented in the *Republic*? Before we speak of a renunciation and of pragmatism, we should note the difference in perspective between the *Republic* and the *Philebus* that forbids our jumping to such conclusions too soon. For one thing, the pedagogical aim of the four sciences (arithmetic, geometry, astronomy, harmonics) in *Republic* VII is to draw the soul out of the Cave to the realm of the really real. It is this aspect that leads to the repudiation of the empirical application of the sciences. In the *Philebus* the pure and applied sciences have already been neatly separated, so Plato can feel comfortable about admitting the applied sciences for everyday purposes, which is his concern here. It stands to reason that Plato would not have denied the necessity of the applied sciences for the purposes of life in the Cave, had that been the focus in the discussion of his educational program.

If it is therefore wrong to speak of a renunciation of purism on Plato's part, nevertheless, there is one major point of difference between the *Republic's* outlook and that of the *Philebus*. First of all, in the later dialogue the good life is depicted as if it were at least in principle attainable for an individual in the here and now.[1] That is the whole point about the harmoni-ous mixture they are looking for. There is not the slightest hint that the successful mixtures discussed by Socrates represent only a shadow existence lit by a dim fire. Nor does the good life consist in flight from the Cave; the good life is lived in this world, in a community that has full

---

1. Plato is silent about the kind of political community that makes possible the right mixture. This silence does not preclude that special conditions must obtain, but the focus here is on the mixture itself.

possession of all the arts and sciences (63a). It is in keeping with this positive attitude to the practical aspects of life that all the arts and sciences have a say in selecting the pleasures that are admitted as part of the good life. For in the *Philebus* not just the philosopher's pleasures of pure thought are regarded as legitimate members, as was forcefully argued in the *Republic* (580d–588a), but all pleasures are admitted that do not interfere with the development and employment of the arts and sciences.

There is danger in comparing and contrasting two dialogues that differ so much in scope and emphasis as the *Republic* and the *Philebus*. But the undeniable fact seems to speak for itself that Plato is letting Socrates turn the search for the good in life into a joint enterprise with a partner who has no philosophical training or pretences, in such a way that they "discover *in the mixture* what the good is in man and in the universe, and get some vision of the nature of the good itself" (64a). The ability to discover the good is not here depicted as the philosopher's privilege, nor is it necessary to turn away from this life to another realm; the criteria enumerated are sufficient to discover the principles of goodness in the mixture. Plato's more conciliatory attitude towards ordinary understanding does not in itself constitute a revision. His intention with the *Philebus* may well have been to show that his conception of the good life can be made intelligible without fully deploying a panoramic political view of the kind divulged in the *Republic* or in the *Laws*. But if the scope and setting of the discussion help to explain the differences in approach, we should not underrate the significance of the *Philebus'* attempt to recommend a life that finds the nonphilosopher's consent. The final 'synthesis' of the mixing together seems to emphasize that it is conceived as a joint effort whose result will be acceptable to everyone not hopelessly committed to the Phileban way of life.

Given the dialogue's more pragmatic approach, does it also represent a change of mind on Plato's part, as far as dialectic is concerned? As mentioned earlier, dialectic is presented in the *Philebus* from two different perspectives that seem prima facie hard to reconcile. The divine method is at first introduced in a way that does not make it necessary to distinguish between the eternal and the temporary; Plato as the dialectician deals with genus and species as well as with the innumerable instances he comes across in his science. But later in the dialogue Plato separates dialectic from all other disciplines and calls it, once again, a "superhuman science." That entities in the physical world can be harmonious mixtures with definite being (albeit mixtures that come and go) suggests that there need be no strict separation between the eternal and the temporal. It would seem that all sciences practice dialectic in the proper fashion if they treat their objects under the aspect of what they *are* rather than how they *come to be* or *perish*. In what sense is this condition fulfilled even by the lowly writing and music teacher, in Plato's examples of the divine method? The writing and music teacher deal with 'divine objects' if they treat their objects as immutable entities and investigate what their *being* consists in. The system of letters or sounds and their relationships is always the same. So the *real* musician is not concerned with the production of individual notes and melodies, but with the timeless relations among them that explain what is a harmonious mixture in music. If the method is divine, so is the object of the science; we need not go to a 'hyperuranious place' to find the divine circle and justice itself. We find them if we apply the gift of the gods in the right way.[1] The difference between a 'divine' and a human science is thus a difference in aspect: The mistake of the "would-be students of nature" Plato addresses (59a) lies not in looking at entities of this world order as such, but in looking at their *temporal conditions*. Individual good mixtures may perish. What does not perish is the principle of what constitutes a good mixture of a certain kind, the relation that must hold between its ingredients.

This basic principle also applies to the dialogue's own subject matter, the good life and its ingredients. Because of this distinction in aspect, Plato can take the partners' joint conception of the good life as a harmonious mixture as the "threshold of the good and the house of every member of its family," as expressed in the passage that leads to the final summary and ranking of goods in our dialogue (64c). A closer analysis of this last passage will have to confirm my claim that Plato's concern in the *Philebus* is with a differentiation in aspect rather than with two rigidly separated worlds, as has often been assumed.[2]

1. This leaves the question of the 'transcendence' of the Forms intact. The obnoxious kind of separation (15a–b) is taken care of, since the 'divine' method allows treating its objects as unchangeable beings, without assuming a 'heaven of ideas'. To work out the most general structure of reality (the connection among the most general Forms) is what is left to dialectic over and above the individual sciences' work.

2. Whether or not this change in approach should be called a *revision* cannot be discussed here. There are no definite criteria to determine when an extension of a theory is no longer an extension but a new theory. The attempt to see radical breaks wherever possible seems just as mistaken as to deny all change in Plato's thought. If the 'revisionists' go too far in one direction in their treatment of the *Philebus*, the 'unitarians' err in the opposite direction; such treatment does not do justice to the ingenuity of this dialogue, cf. Waterfield (1980) and Hampton (1990).

V. The solution of the discussion:
the final ranking of all goods (64c–end).

The way to answer the remaining question concerning the good, *viz.*
determining the decisive factor in the good mixture and what comes closest
to it, has of course been paved early on by the fourfold division. But as
Protarchus is unable to sum up the result in general terms, Socrates once
again assumes that task: The success of every mixture depends on the
right measure and proportion of its ingredients.[1] The key terms measure
(*metron*) and proportion (*symmetron*) provide him with further associations,
so that he can claim that the good has taken refuge in a conjunction
of three forms, *beauty, proportion,* and *truth.*[2] What is the point of this
diversification of the notion of the good? Since Socrates is going to show,
with Protarchus' enthusiastic consent, that reason is superior on all three
counts, one may think that the reasons for characterizing the good as a
threesome are mainly rhetorical, so that reason appears in the glory of a
triple victory. But if such a rhetorical flourish is not unintentional, it can
hardly be Plato's only motive. For all three terms have been employed as
criteria of evaluation in the critique of pleasure and knowledge. Now the
criteria are applied to the mixture itself, not just its ingredients. So Socrates
is right in emphasizing the need for proportion, i.e., the right *balance*
between pleasure and knowledge, the elements that constitute the good
life. What does beauty have to do with a well-balanced life? We should
remember that the Greek word *kalon* means not only aesthetically pleasing
but also morally admirable. So the demand is that the right kind of life is
aesthetically as well as morally pleasing. There is a similar kind of ambiguity in the word "truth," which can mean both literal truth and truthfulness.
The good life is true because it not only contains true elements of pleasure
and knowledge but also is a life of trustworthiness. And measure or
proportion is also understood as moderation. As we can see from Protarchus' replies, this seems to be the spirit in which he at least understands
the final test that pleasure and knowledge have to undergo to determine
where they belong on the scale of goods.

This discussion may not exhaust Plato's reasons for presenting the final

---

1. The mathematical aspect of the theory is limited to such bare indications, but it explains
why Plato insists on a special role for this discipline.

2. Truth has been the explicit criterion all along; though some compromise turns out to be
necessary with regard to truth and purity in the final mixture, they insure the mixture's
stability (61e–62a). Measure and beauty were claimed especially for the pure pleasures (51c;
52c).

criterion of goodness as a threesome, but it should draw attention to the fact that goodness itself has not been defined as a unified concept. Its relatedness to measure and all that possesses moderation has been emphasized throughout the dialogue, but no further attempt is made at capturing goodness itself. So the indication that the partners need three criteria to make goodness 'operable' for the final selection points to that omission, which becomes all the more poignant if we remember that the good was on the original list of cases whose unity is a matter of serious controversy (15a). Plato quite clearly wants to limit the scope of the discussion in the *Philebus* to settling the initial question whether reason is a better good than pleasure.

Given the tenor of the critique of pleasure and knowledge, it is only to be expected that reason wins over pleasure on all counts. If there is anything interesting in this summary of the competition, it lies in the fact that Protarchus' evaluations seem rather crude. When he admits pleasure's inferiority in terms of moderation, trustworthiness, and seemliness, he cites the grosser kinds of pleasures (the excessive joys of sex seem foremost in his mind). Did he not realize that those have already been banished from the good life? Does Plato want to indicate that Protarchus, despite all his good will and patience, has not learned a thing from Socrates about the real meaning of the limit, the unlimited, and their combination?

There are, of course, several factors about Protarchus that shed doubt on the extent of his conversion to a Socratic point of view; not least among them is the fact that he reaffirms his allegiance to Gorgias rather late in the dialogue (58a–b). But if Plato lets him reassert his rather conventional moral ideas, this shows only that the discussion has not led to a miraculous character change. Plato never overplays his cards in making converts out of Socrates' partners; no one ever ends as a full convert who does not have leanings in that direction right from the beginning. The way Protarchus is presented is in keeping with this practice. So Plato is content to prove a point, which he can prove with some plausibility, that even a man quite subject to the fashions of his day can be made to see the incoherence of hedonism, provided he is willing to listen to argument. Only the unreasoning hedonist of Philebus' ilk cannot be convinced. He has been silent for a long time and remains so to the end of the dialogue.

Once the superiority of reason over pleasure has been established, the goods are lined up in a final ranking: First comes measure, followed by harmonious ("measured") mixtures; reason and intelligence obtain third place; the less pure arts and sciences together with true belief come fourth; and pure pleasures obtain fifth place. If the list presents some difficulties, they vanish if one keeps it in mind that it lists the goods that make up a good *human* life. It is not a metaphysical ranking of everything there is in the universe, although one might, of course, try to extrapolate from it to such an all-encompassing ranking.[1] That the ingredients of the good human life are at stake here explains, for instance, the distinction between the prime good, measure, and the secondary good, the measured; and it explains why pure reason and intelligence obtain only third place. The proper *balance* between all ingredients must come first, and then the life that incorporates them, including all the harmonious mixtures such a life contains, such as virtue, health, a just society, etc. Since (human) reason is the cause of this mixture, it comes only third.[2] The distinction between the more and less precise sciences will have prepared us for the separation of reason (*nous*) and intelligence (*phronesis*) from the lesser disciplines. That their practical application is what counts in the ranking of the lower sciences is confirmed by the inclusion of true *doxa* in this class. We cannot do without beliefs about the contingent conditions in life. Nor should we be surprised that only the pure pleasures, those of both the intellect and the senses, make it to the rank of the good: They are the only ones not mixed with pain (51a–53c). Some commentators have suggested a sixth rank for the necessary pleasures, because Socrates' quotation of the Orphic verse seems ambiguous (66c8–9). But since, in reconfirming the final result that pleasure is the lowest kind of good (67a14), Socrates speaks only of a fifth rank, such speculation appears groundless.

In his peroration Socrates drives home his complete victory over hedonism: Only animals and those who take animals as their cue would vote for a life of pleasure rather than a life of inspiration by the "philosophic muse." Although Philebus is not named, clearly he is finally discredited as the man of animal passions whose erstwhile friend and spokesman Protarchus forsakes him by unreservedly accepting this result.

The dialogue actually ends on a somewhat surprising note. When Socrates asks for final release from his task, Protarchus claims that "there is still a little missing." So the discussion does not really end, just as it had no proper beginning. Should we regard this as an ironic indication that much more than "a little" is missing, or should we take it as a sign that Protarchus is so converted to Socrates' point of view that he cannot

---

1. The macrocosm-microcosm analogy discussed earlier invites such extrapolation, and Socrates hints at a wider perspective at 64a.

2. Socrates' distinction between his own *nous* and divine reason (22c) is to be remembered here.

get enough? It it difficult to decide how much weight to give to this remark, but the "little that is left" should give rise to fruitful speculation. Protarchus may refer to the fact that they have not said anything about *how* the good life is actually to be lived. And behind that question larger questions loom. The "final grading" in particular presents a problem not treated in the *Philebus* at all, namely, what the "measure" of the mixture consists in and how to find it. In our dialogue, the notion of measure or limit remains a postulate. It must be there if the requisite successful combination of limit and unlimitedness is to be achieved. But none of these explanations tells us in the least what the right measure for each successful mixture would be and how we could determine it. We have reached the "threshold of the good" but have gone no further, for although we have seen the *function* of the good in human life, we do not know how to determine what it ought to contain. To go beyond this threshold would be a tall order. There are a great many harmonious mixtures, not only in the universe at large but also in human life. To find them means to apply *limit* to the manifold unlimitedness. How are we to determine the right limit, the measure and proportion? The full program hinted at in the macrocosm-microcosm analogy points in two directions. On the one hand it points to the need for a full-scale cosmology to find the key to the harmonious mixtures in nature. On the other it emphasizes the need to analyze the content of the right kind of human life and its conditions. Such studies will reveal the right measures to us, as far as this is humanly possible. So our dialogue seems to be a preface to two other late Platonic works: the cosmology of the *Timaeus*, and the ideal social life as described in the *Laws*.[1] What a right mixture is and how it comes about is a long story, or so it would seem.

3. The Socratic question: the dialogue's form.

The most crucial question concerning Plato's intentions in the whole dialogue can be put into four words: Why is Socrates back? The obvious answer to this question was suggested earlier: The *topic*, the rivalry between pleasure and knowledge as the supreme good in human life, occupied Socrates a great deal in Plato's earlier work. We may add some further considerations. Not only is it an old topic, but the whole concern is typically Socratic, for the question of the good *human* life may be called

---

1. This does not prejudice the actual chronological order of those works. For a brief discussion of points of similarity between *Philebus* and *Timaeus*, cf. Hackforth (1954), 2–3.

the Socratic question *par excellence*. In addition, the procedure satisfies Socratic demands: To determine whether pleasure or knowledge are good, we have to find out what pleasure and knowledge (in all their varieties) *are*. The Socrates of old would have pressed this question: "How can we know whether pleasure or knowledge is a good, if we do not know what they are, in and of themselves?" Where the Socratic approach in the *Philebus* differs is in clearly showing that a one-line definition, to be prodded and tested by questioning, is not possible. Only the proper application of the method of dialectic, the "gift of the gods," will be sufficient to accomplish that.

If these arguments look like sufficient justification for a Socratic renaissance, they are by no means the only ones. There is also the dialogue's form, which goes back to Socratic practices. Socrates may not be as amusingly aggressive as he is in some early dialogues; but such aggressiveness already had been left behind in most of the middle dialogues. Glaucon's critique at the beginning of the second book of the *Republic*, to the effect that combat-style discussions lead only to nominal victories, not real convictions, presents a kind of watershed. So the Socrates of the *Philebus* acts quite in agreement with that change in Plato's conception of how a philosophical debate should be conducted. If the scene is not as richly drawn as it is in the *Symposium*, the *Phaedo*, or the *Phaedrus*, certainly the interaction of Socrates with his partners is lively enough. The partners appear as real persons and Socrates treats them as such, witness the marked difference in the way he deals with Philebus and with Protarchus. Protarchus himself, although not the most dramatically developed personality of all of Socrates' partners, is nevertheless a genuine partner to the discussion. He is not at all comparable to the 'answering machines' that we find in other late Platonic dialogues (cf. the young Socrates' stand-in called Aristoteles in the second part of the *Parmenides*, Theaetetus in the *Sophist*, the younger Socrates in the *Statesman*). Protarchus participates in a most active way, and even Philebus is drawn back into the discussion at various points, if only to signal grudging curiosity or overall discontent.

So we may conclude with some confidence that active cooperation is a necessary condition when deciding the proper human life. Plato must have felt that a "lecture" in the style of the *Timaeus* would be inappropriate for this purpose. The decision of what kind of life is worth living is not left to an expert's discretion here, because Socrates wants to find the kind of life acceptable to anyone capable of and willing to engage in cooperative debate. Such is not a life of high-minded intellectuals only. It is a life that mixes pleasure with knowledge, so that even an unreflective hedonist of ordinary convictions, a devoted disciple of Gorgias, can accept it as better than a life of pleasure pure and simple. This aim may explain why the discussion in the *Philebus* in many ways recalls Socrates' discussion style of the earlier dialogues rather than his expository style of the *Republic*. If Plato initially makes Protarchus seem like a weaker edition of Callicles in the *Gorgias*, this is by intention, and is not a sign that in his old age he had grown weary of the dramatic demands of dialogue as such. He is no longer interested in confrontational discussions, which merely leave Socrates' opponents unconvinced and angry—and force Socrates to conclude his discussions himself. The stubborn hedonist is therefore put aside straightaway as incapable of dialogue. The average person of hedonistic inclinations, by contrast, can be made to see the crucial point about the mixed life: There is an ideal form of life that combines both reason and pleasure. And this partner remains with Socrates to the end of the debate.

If this explains why Plato gave Protarchus the kind of personality he did, we are left with a question about the result of the dialogue. Is Socrates' return some sort of recantation, at least where the highest form of human life is concerned, so that Socrates turns out to quite agree with Everyman Protarchus? Does a quiet renunciation of the need for an expert in the decision over the best human life represent so fundamental a change that Plato had to bring Socrates back to show he really meant it? The foregoing analysis of the dialogue has pointed up a kind of ambiguity in Socrates' attitude. On one hand, it is hardly doubtful that he shares the compromise solution about the good life that he urges Protarchus to accept. On the other hand, there are always those indications about the *really* best state: the divine state of completeness where pleasure has no place, the divine method, the divine science, the divine circle. Without dialectic no verdict could have been reached to decide the case of pleasure vs. knowledge.

I have suggested that this ambiguity is not really an inconsistency; it only points out that the really perfect state is not one that human beings can attain, although it might be the state we should aspire to as much as we can. Nor is this an un-Socratic position to adopt. Although it must seem un-Socratic if we compare it with Socrates' recommendation to flee this world altogether in the *Phaedo*, it quite agrees with the message of the lecture in the *Symposium*: that humans are forever in-between creatures, between the mortal and immortal, the finite and infinite, the good and bad. It also agrees with the picture of life worked out further in the *Phaedrus*, where love is exploited as a pedagogical device that draws us after the gods but does not make us into gods. So here Plato seems to recall Socrates, son of Poros and Penia, the mighty demon and hunter for truth, who discusses the kind of life that does justice to man's situation between a purely earthly and a divine condition. If the tone of the discussion is less inspired and less inspiring, the explanation is that the partner shows less spirit than Phaedrus does, or than does Socrates himself, the disciple of Diotima in matters of love.

There is, of course, nothing strange about such a Socratic renaissance, especially if it gives Plato the opportunity to revise some details in his earlier critique of pleasure and its relation to knowledge as goods to which everyone might aspire. Nor is it strange that Plato should have returned to the topic after many years, if he felt the need to make some corrections while reaffirming his overall stance. That he lends Socrates the tools of his more developed method of dialectic is not surprising either. He must have found it important to show what these tools can do when brought to bear on the question of the good life.

But this explanation of the revival of a partly identical and partly refurbished Socrates, designed to prove the continuity in Platonic ethics, is not the whole story. We should also remember that the Socrates of the *Philebus* has clearly profited from the lesson he was taught by old Parmenides. The 'divine method' is introduced as a way out of the difficulties with the Forms. It closes the gap between the transcendent, immobile, separate unity of the Forms and the ever changeable plurality of sensible objects. So Socrates' reappearance has another purpose: It indicates that the theory of the Forms has survived all criticism. Of particular importance, and a sign of careful planning on Plato's part, is that he lets an older Socrates explain the difficulties once again and indicate that they are capable of solution. This last explanation of Socrates' reappearance is in a sense also the most problematic, since, as already indicated, this aspect of the dialogue remains very much a matter of speculation. Socrates has carried out only a limited program in the search for the good. He has not exploited the full potential of the divine method in that search, so one cannot help wondering whether these unmistakable limitations demonstrate the limitations of the Socratic approach even where un-Socratic means are employed. Despite all hunches and divine help, Socrates does not go beyond the search for the human good. Beyond that border, the real work in the search for the good is yet to be done. And that will presumably once again be the work of an expert who is not tied down by the necessary limits of cooperation. By virtue of all these limiting conditions, this particular occasion permitted a truly Socratic discussion, which explains why it is the only discussion in Plato's late works where Socrates speaks.

So Socrates is back because he is dealing with a Socratic question with a Socratic partner with the aid of Platonic tools. Plato gives clear indications that the tools are not Socrates'. Whenever something clearly un-Socratic is assumed, he indicates that fact. There is not only the gift of the gods, or the sudden dreamlike brainstorm, but also the explicit attribution to other sources, such as the 'harsh antihedonist' or the 'subtle thinkers'. Yet all these indications do not detract from but rather enhance the importance of Socrates' return. The un-Socratic elements in the dialogue notwithstanding, Plato obviously wanted to emphasize the importance of making Socrates himself the spokesman of this new conception of the good human life, as a life that an audience of ordinary Athenian youths can accept, provided they are willing to engage in a real conversation. One cannot reform a Callicles or a Philebus, so it is better not to try. But one can get far with those who, like Protarchus, are ready to listen.

4. The question concerning Eudoxus.

So far we have discussed only internal reasons in the development of Plato's own thought to explain why he thoroughly overhauled the concepts of pleasure and knowledge as determining factors of human life. There may also have been external factors that made him dedicate a whole dialogue to this old problem after so many years. One such external factor, often mentioned in the secondary literature, was the defense of a hedonistic position by Eudoxus, the most famous mathematician and astronomer of his age, whose innovations in these areas seem to have considerably influenced Plato in the *Timaeus*.[1] That this contact with Eudoxus led to renewed debate on the nature and value of pleasure is confirmed by Aristotle's discussion of the notion of pleasure in his *Nicomachean Ethics*, where the position of Eudoxus is briefly summarized alongside other views (Book 10, 1172b9–25; an even shorter summary is contained in Book 7, 1153b25–31). Aristotle in fact seems to present Plato's position as an answer to Eudoxus' contention that pleasure is the only good. If he was not himself an eyewitness to that debate, he may well have drawn on a source that reported a debate among members of the

---

1. Gosling (1975) emphasizes the influence of Eudoxus throughout his commentary. For a survey of other scholarly work on Eudoxus, cf. Lasserre, *Die Fragmente des Eudoxos von Knidos*, Berlin (1966), 151–156.

Academy which was stirred by Eudoxus' challenge.[1] From Aristotle's report we can conclude that there was the pro-pleasure faction of Eudoxus, and an anti-pleasure faction headed by Plato's nephew and successor Speusippus. Other mixed positions are mentioned but no names given apart from references to Plato's own theory of pleasure.

Since Eudoxus was in Athens around 360 and stood in close contact with Plato and other members of the Academy,[2] it is quite likely that his unrestricted endorsement of hedonism started a heated debate that prompted Plato to take a second look at his own earlier conception of pleasure. He thus came to revise certain aspects of the views he had expressed in the ninth book of the *Republic* (580d ff.). A renewed general interest in hedonism would explain why Plato took up that question again after so many years. But whether Eudoxus was more than a catalyst to the debate in Plato's dialogue seems questionable. First of all, he was not a philosopher who focused on ethics, nor is he often called a philosopher at all.[3] In addition, Aristotle's report suggests that Eudoxus' hedonistic view cannot have been based on a very elaborate theory. "His arguments were credited more because of the excellence of his character than for their own sake; he was thought to be remarkably self-controlled, and therefore it was thought that he was not saying what he did say as a friend of pleasure, but that the facts were really so (1172b15–18)." So the most impressive point about his arguments seems to have been that they were not a glutton's self-serving statements but the pronouncements of a man of sober character. All this speaks for the assumption that there was not much of theory behind his position. There are, for instance, no reports on a definition or further differentiation of Eudoxus' notion of pleasure. Nor does it seem that Eudoxus' one other reported philosophical achievement would have presented much of a challenge to Plato; the rudimentary

---

1. Lasserre suggests that Eudoxus' position was probably not presented in written form, but as an oral contribution in the debate; a record of that debate on pleasure by Speusippus may have been Aristotle's source as well as the source of later references to Eudoxus' position. This conjecture may well be right, for though Aristotle's discussion contains a reply to Plato's conception of pleasure as a *genesis* or as a process (*EN* 10, ch. 3), he does not go into the *Philebus'* debate in any detail, nor does his discussion follow the logical order of the dialogue.

2. The ancient reports on the dates of Eudoxus' life diverge widely. There is still no consensus, but most scholars agree that he must have lived from roughly 390 to 340 B.C.

3. Eudoxus is usually addressed as an astronomer, geometer, doctor, and lawgiver (cf. *D.L.* 8 86). This agrees well with the fact that reports on his astronomical and mathematical achievements are very rich, while there are very scanty fragments on his philosophical doctrine.

theory of Forms he is credited with seems to provide a quite simplistic justification for immanent Forms.[1]

The actual position on pleasure's goodness which Aristotle ascribes to him suggests that he took a naturalist's stance. He seems to have favored pleasure as the supreme good on the ground of the 'argument from nature's voice': Each thing naturally finds its own good, just as it finds its own nourishment (1172b13–4). The same argument that speaks for the natural goodness of pleasure is also used to show that pain is the natural evil. Pain is what all seek to avoid; it must therefore be a natural evil. Eudoxus seems to have crowned his plea for the goodness of pleasure with the claim that pleasure must be a supreme good because it is sought as an ultimate aim, not as a means to further goods. If this sums up Eudoxus' position, his must have been more a common sense view on pleasure than a proper philosophical theory. For although Aristotle is sympathetic to his basic principle that what all aspire to must indeed be good, and regards its denial as quite perverse and foolish (1172b35–1173ab5), he is clearly not overly impressed by Eudoxus' reasoning as a whole.

If Aristotle's impression of Eudoxus' position is right, Plato cannot have regarded him as a formidable spokesman for hedonism, although the renewed debate in the Academy may have prompted him to review the whole issue. But though Eudoxus' position may have had little direct impact on Plato's reconsiderations in reaction to that debate, the dialogue refers to Eudoxus' position on the naturalness of pleasure at least in one important respect. Plato's new, unified definition of pleasure as the 'restoration of the natural equilibrium' is a kind of reply to Eudoxus' argument 'from nature's voice'. If there is something natural in all creatures' quest for pleasure, Plato seems to reply, it is because all animals stand in constant need of restoration. So pleasure is, at its very best, only a *remedial natural* good. All pleasures that are not restorations of a natural lack (whether felt or unfelt) are to be avoided; they cannot be regarded as a good at all. The ontological niche that Plato has found for pleasure as a kind of restoration gives him an apt reply to Eudoxus' challenge that

---

1. Aristotle indicates why it was easily refuted (*Met.* A 991a14), and Alexander of Aphrodisias in his commentary refers to some of the arguments familiar already from Plato's *Parmenides* against Eudoxus' crude theory of "participation" (*CAG* 1, Berlin 1891, 97, 17–98, 24). If his theory originated at a later date than Plato's dialogue, this proves not only that Eudoxus was not much of a philosopher, but also that he had a quite superficial knowledge of Platonic metaphysics.

pleasure is the highest good in nature. The basic notion, however, was already discussed in the *Republic*, where pleasure is presented as a kind of 'filling of a lack', so he had only to refurbish and elaborate on that old conception when he subsumed pleasure under the genus of the 'unlimited'. Since the ontological determination of the nature of pleasure and pain was Plato's most serious concern in the *Philebus*, the debate stirred up by Eudoxus' challenge can indeed have been no more than a catalyst. As this essay has suggested, Plato had plenty of internal reasons to rework his old theory that have nothing to do with Eudoxus.

Are there further traces of Eudoxan influence in the *Philebus*, besides the challenge concerning pleasure's natural goodness? The case for a much wider influence by Eudoxus on Plato has been forcefully argued in Gosling's commentary (1975) on the *Philebus*.[1] This is not the place for a thorough review of this claim and the evidence it is based on, because it would involve a detailed discussion; for Gosling also regards all Pythagorean elements in the *Philebus* and the emphasis on a *limit* in terms of measure and number as the result of Eudoxus' influence. He holds, for instance, that the realization of the impossibility of expressing everything in terms of relations of rational integers is the rationale behind Plato's choice of *apeiron* as a genus.

The problem with attributing all the Pythagoreanizing to the influence of Eudoxus is that Plato was well familiar with Pythagoreanism long before Eudoxus came to Athens. In addition, while Pythagorean influence on the musical theory divulged in the *Philebus* is very likely, it is difficult to see how such a mathematical approach can be applied in the dialectical schema of the divine method in general. It already does not seem to work for Plato's other example besides the notes of music, i.e., the classification of letters in the story of the discovery of Theuth. It is highly implausible that Plato should have conceived of the sounds we produce in speech as analogous to the way notes in music are produced by the harmonious division of the string on a monochord.[2]

1. Gosling treats the desirability criterion at 20d as a sign of Eudoxan influence, 87–88; 139–142. That pleasure is insufficient as a good is "tailored to Eudoxus' position" (167), because at 20 ff. Plato turns his argument against him that pleasure always increases the goodness of whatever it is added to.

2. For a critical discussion of the mathematical influence of Eudoxus on the metaphysics of the *Philebus*, cf. the review of Gosling's commentary by G.E.R. Lloyd, *Classical Review* 27 (1977), 173–75. According to Lloyd, Gosling exaggerates the influence of Eudoxus, because Plato seems unaware of his major achievement, the extension of the theory of proportion to incommensurables. Lloyd also finds the interpretation of *apeiron* and *peras* at 16a ff. and at

Gosling grants that Philebus, as a person, "hardly represents Eudoxus, but he does represent the repercussions of Eudoxus," (141). This ignores the fact that Philebus is presented as the very glutton that Eudoxus, according to Aristotle's praise of his character, was not. If Plato chose Philebus as the prototype of the hedonist, he must have wanted to make clear that he is not attacking Eudoxus, unless he meant the dialogue as a kind of shock therapy to demonstrate that hedonism is 'pig-philosophy'. Matters are not much mended if we try to substitute Protarchus for Eudoxus. For though Protarchus is not as obsessed as his friend Philebus with pleasure of the crudest kind, he well represents Socrates' usual audience, the ordinary wealthy young Athenian who has to be weaned from the influence of the sophists. A man like Eudoxus would have needed no such weaning, nor would he have had as hard a time understanding Socrates' references to mathematics as Protarchus does. That it is the ordinary hedonist whom Socrates tries to win over to his view of the good in life should warn us not to make too much of the Eudoxan influence.

5. The 'esoteric' Plato.

Plato never tells us all he thinks and knows, and often we must doubt whether he tells us what he thinks at all. Most of the time we finish a dialogue with a heightened understanding of the problems discussed, rather than with a firm conviction that we know Plato's own solution to them, or that the apparent solution in a dialogue is really his last word on the question. Often the indications of solutions remain mere indications. In addition, Plato never speaks in his own name, and we cannot be sure to what extent he agrees with his protagonist, even when the protagonist is Socrates. Our uncertainty thus also extends to the elaborate discussions of the *Republic* and the *Laws*. These facts, in conjunction with Plato's expressed critical stance towards writing as a means of expressing philosophical thought[1] has led to quite different schools of thought on Plato. On one side stand those who recommend that despite all uncertainty we can do no better than stick to the dialogues themselves and, where neces-

---

23a ff. too restrictive as an account of *techne* and its products. The 'fine mixtures' in nature cannot be conceived as products of *techne*.

1. The central text is *Phaedrus* (276b–278c); the same reservations are expressed in the *Seventh Letter* (341a–345c), the latter with an explicit reference to Plato's own teaching.

sary, read between or behind the lines.[1] On the other side stand those who argue that the 'real Plato' is not to be found in the dialogues, or is found there only incompletely. This school of thought assumes that, as a matter of principle, certain issues were not discussed by Plato in the dialogues but conveyed to the inner circle of his disciples in oral discussions. Some traces of such 'esoteric' discussions seem to have survived in reports on Plato in antiquity which give supplementary information concerning doctrine not found in the dialogues. Hence the need to thoroughly sift through the remaining relics of that esoteric teaching. This line of thought has had its attractions throughout history, from antiquity on. Its justification is very much a matter of debate.[2] The assumption of an oral tradition in Plato received its name from a remark in Aristotle's *Physics* (4, 209b15), where Aristotle attributes a certain view on matter and space to so-called unwritten doctrines, *agrapha dogmata*, of Plato. So talk of 'unwritten doctrine' goes back to a very ancient source.

The reports used to justify the claim of an esoteric doctrine for Plato start with Aristotle's critique of Plato's theory of Forms, which refers us to a version of that theory that does not readily agree with what we find in Plato's dialogues themselves. It rather seems to put Plato close to Pythagorean conceptions, both in content and in terminology. The most prominent text is chapter 6 of Aristotle's *Metaphysics* A.[3] According to this passage Plato assumed two basic principles, the *one* and an *indefinite duality*; these principles are said to be the elements of Forms as well as of their sensible counterparts. Mathematical objects are between sensibles and Forms, but 'the one' is the ultimate cause of all Forms as well as of all goodness. The details in Aristotle's account are difficult to penetrate, and this brief summary must suffice for our purposes. The question of their meaning and relation to Plato's philosophy is thus still a matter of debate.

What strengthens the belief in such an unwritten doctrine is the supplementary information from the sixth century commentator Simplicius, in

1. Its most uncompromising representative is H. Cherniss; for a brief and lucid discussion, cf. Cherniss (1945).

2. For a survey of this development from the revival of Platonic studies in the nineteenth century, cf. Cherniss (1945). Despite Cherniss' energetic attempts to show the groundlessness of this approach, it has been forcefully taken up again in the last thirty years by the members of the so-called Tübingen school, cf. Gaiser (1980); for a compromise position, cf. J. N. Findley (1974).

3. 987b10–988a17; cf. also the report in *Metaph*. M 4. For further discussion, cf. W.D. Ross, *Aristotle Metaphysics*, Oxford 1958, vol. I, 157–177.

his commentary on Aristotle's *Physics*.[1] Simplicius associates this Platonic theory, which largely agrees with the summary in Aristotle's *Metaphysics*, with Plato's "Lecture on the Good," a lecture that seems to have puzzled more than enlightened not only the wider public that attended but also Plato's own students. For each of them, according to Simplicius, made notes on that occasion. That such a lecture took place is confirmed by another source much earlier than Simplicius. Aristoxenus, a disciple of Aristotle who lived at the end of the fourth century B.C., reports with some relish that the lecture was a flop, because Plato did not speak on the kinds of goods the public was expecting but rather on mathematics, numbers, geometry, astronomy, and the unity of goodness.[2] If there was such an event, which we have no good reason to doubt, then it is important to register that even Plato's disciples had difficulty understanding what Plato said, as Simplicius acknowledges when he speaks of its "enigmatic" character (453,30).

One may wonder what the "unwritten doctrines" have to do with the *Philebus* and why we should bother opening this can of worms here. The reason is that a kind of middle position exists between the textual purists on Plato, who acknowledge no other source of information, and the esotericists, who assume that certain doctrines were not put into the dialogues as a matter of principle. This 'middle position' claims that the alleged unwritten doctrines can be traced back to the *Philebus*. If this is right, the *Philebus* is the missing link between the reports on Plato that seemingly have no basis in the dialogues and the dialogues themselves. It seems especially significant for reconstructing this relation between the unwritten doctrines and the content of the *Philebus* that such a connection, according to Simplicius, had been advocated by Porphyry in his commentary on the *Philebus* itself.

What kind of relation to Plato's *Philebus* can be constructed on the basis of our gleanings from Aristotle and Simplicius? There emerges a closer affinity between this alleged Platonic doctrine of two principles, the "one" and the "indefinite duality" (*aoristos dyas*), and the fourfold ontological division of the *Philebus* (the limit, the unlimited, their mixture, and its cause), if we take into account what is meant by the indefinite duality. Aristotle also calls the indefinite duality "unlimited" and explains it in terms of "the great and the small" (987b20–27). Simplicius adds further explanations familiar from the *Philebus*; besides "the great and the small"

---

1. *CAG* vol. 9, (ed.) H. Diels, Berlin 1882, 453, 19–455,14.
2. Cf. *The Harmonics of Aristoxenos* (ed.) H.S. Macran, Oxford 1902, 30–31.

he also uses the expression "more and less," as well as "strongly and gently" (453,32–3). So it seems that the 'indefinite dyad', the second of Plato's alleged basic principles, is regarded as identical with the *apeiron* of the *Philebus* and taken to share its definition of what allows for the more and less. What is emphasized in making it a 'duality' is that the underlying medium is always indeterminate in two directions: As long as it does not take on a limit, a definite ratio, there can be always *more* in quantity and there can be *less*.[1]

Since the 'unlimited' in the *Philebus* plays a role both on the level of the Forms and on the level of sensible particulars, as we have seen, we are not surprised that Plato presented it as such in his lecture "On the Good" and spoke about mathematics, cosmology, and the *unity* of goodness. Although 'limit' is not ultimately reduced to oneness in the *Philebus*, such an identification is not difficult to construe. The right limit always constitutes the unity of everything that can accept it, both among the Forms themselves and among their sensible instances, so that 'limit' stands for unity. For limit as the right measure or proportion is the principle that makes integrated wholes or units out of otherwise unstable medleys. Any good mixture consists in a harmonious equilibrium of its otherwise indeterminate ingredients, the high and low, the warm and cold, or whatever the basic stratum may be. It is true that there is no talk of unity in the *Philebus*, besides the unity of the Forms (15a–b). But then, the dialogue never enlightens us about the character of the ultimate unity of the four highest genera of being. Our dialogue confines itself to a rough general outline. Plato's silence there does not mean, however, that he had no more to tell.

That the 'fourfold division' was not more clearly relevant for understanding the lecture "On the Good" and that Plato seems to have created the impression instead that all Forms are numbers should not disturb us too much, given the topic of that lecture. It was a lecture on the good, so it must have focused on good mixtures and their principles, i.e., the right ratios among their ingredients, expressed in terms of numbers. The fourfold division in the *Philebus*, as interpreted in this essay, suggests that

---

1. H. Jackson (1882) was the first in modern times to comment extensively on this connection between the *Philebus* and the 'unwritten doctrine'. Others have followed him, cf. Hackforth (1945), 37–43, and most recently Sayre (1984), ch. 3, "The *Philebus* and the Good." Sayre is very positive about a direct connection between the *Philebus* and Plato's lecture "On the Good"; he identifies the Forms with the numbers of successful mixtures, however, and does not sufficiently explain what justifies treating only one of Plato's four classes of being as containing Forms.

there are other kinds of Forms, or Forms of other kinds of beings, not just Forms of good things. But this issue may not have come up for further discussion in Plato's lecture, if all that falls in the genus of the unlimited was summarily treated under the heading of 'indefinite dyad' and dismissed from further talk about goodness. To those not familiar with the sense of that terminology, it must have seemed as if all Forms consisted in numbers, pure and simple.

Why did Plato have difficulty making himself understood in his lecture "On the Good" if the *Philebus*' fourfold division of all beings forms the background of what he wanted to convey? We cannot presume to unravel the mysteries around this lecture, but this much we may conjecture: The doctrine of the *Philebus* is difficult enough to understand, even with the illustrations and explanations provided in the dialogue. If Plato in his lecture spoke on an even higher level of abstraction, as the reports on that event suggest, then he must have been unintelligible to all those who had not thoroughly immersed themselves beforehand in the 'fourfold division of being' and speculated on its possible wider applications.

Why even Plato's students seem to have comprehended so little of their teacher's intentions in that respect must remain an open question, it seems. An answer would presuppose more information than we have about the kind of exchange that took place in the Academy. If there really was a relationship between the *Philebus* and the lecture, it seems that Plato's students could have grasped more had they studied the *Philebus* more closely and asked Plato more questions about it.[1] Why did they not do that? Given the time it takes to penetrate a text like the *Philebus*, it is easy to see why they did not. Had Aristotle spent as much time on it as seems necessary to us, his career would have been different. He would not have become Aristotle but Plato's first commentator. Philosophers with their own agenda are hardly ever good commentators on their predecessors, as the history of philosophy confirms; if they have an ax to grind, they hardly take the time and patience to immerse themselves sufficiently in the texts they refer to. Impatience with the predecessor's work explains many historical misrepresentations. In Plato's case, as we have seen, the problem was aggravated by the style of his writing. Even if he did not intentionally cloak his dialogues' meaning, he may not have been ready to answer the

---

1. Cf. Sayre, 174. Aristotle's critique of Plato's conception of pleasure in the *Nicomachean Ethics* (10, 1173a15–b20) suggests that he knew the *Philebus* fairly well, but he may well have used Speusippus' doxographical report on concepts of pleasure as his immediate source, as mentioned before, cf. p. lxxiin1.

questions of those who had not invested enough work to penetrate the difficulties beforehand. Given those difficulties, students all too often may not have been in a position to raise the relevant questions. That explains why they often do not seem to know more than we do, despite their proximity to their master and teacher.

From this brief summary, it emerges that the *Philebus* is indeed a crucial text for understanding the 'riddle of the Academy' and the enigma that was Plato's lecture "On the Good." But what use is there in studying the tangled question of an 'esoteric teaching' of Plato for our understanding of the *Philebus* itself? The payoff in that direction is indeed only indirect.[1] We do not get any information from these later reports that is not more readily available from studying the dialogue itself. But they confirm that the *Philebus* is essential for understanding Plato's late ontology and that it was understood to be so by at least some of his later commentators. Although the *Philebus* was never one of the most popular writings, it always had its friends and was regarded as a key text at different times in the afterlife of Platonism, as we can see from the extant commentaries.[2] This much must suffice as a brief summary of the problems concerning an 'esoteric Plato' and the muted impact of the *Philebus*.

1. Cf. Hampton's complaints (1990), 95–101.

2. For ancient sources, cf. Westerink (1959); for Marsilio Ficino and his interpretation, cf. M. J. B. Allan (1975).

Plato

Philebus[1]

The persons and the setting of the dialogue:
Socrates, Protarchus, Philebus

Nothing is known of Philebus, and some interpreters regard him as purely fictional (the name, "youth-lover", is almost too good to be true for a real-life hedonist who is at the same time the spoilt beauty, the center of a circle of admirers). Protarchus is addressed as "son of Callias" once. Since he professes allegiance to the sophist Gorgias, he is in all likelihood one of the two sons of Callias, one of the richest men of Athens, who, as Plato lets Socrates say in the *Apology* (20a), "spent more than anyone else on the sophists." No indications are given as to the location or the fictional date of the dialogue, except that Socrates is older than the group of youths he is conversing with.

I. The introductory challenge:
pleasure vs. knowledge (11a–14b)

Soc.: Well, then, Protarchus, consider just what the thesis is that you are now taking over from Philebus—and what *our* thesis is that you are going to argue against, if you find that you do not agree with it. Shall we summarize them both? 11

Pro.: Yes, let's do that.

Soc.: Philebus holds that what is good for all creatures is to enjoy themselves, to be pleased and delighted, and whatever else goes together with that kind of thing.[2] We contend that not these, but knowing, understanding, and remembering, and what belongs with them, right opinion and true calculations, are better than pleasure and more agreeable to all who

b

x

c

---

1. If not otherwise indicated, the Greek text used is the J. Burnet edition, Oxford 1901. Where readings suggested by A. Diès (edition Budé, Platon, *Oeuvres complètes*, vol. IX, Paris 1949) have been preferred, the translation is marked with an asterisk (*).

2. The expression leaves open whether pleasure is *the* good or *a* good. In the ensuing discussion it becomes clear that the former is meant (cf. 60a).

can attain them;[1] those who can, get the maximum benefit possible from having them, both those now alive and future generations. Isn't that how we present our respective positions, Philebus?

PHI.: Absolutely, Socrates.

SOC.: Do you agree, Protarchus, to take over this thesis that's now offered you?

PRO.: I am afraid I have to. Fair Philebus has given up on us.

SOC.: So we must do everything possible to get through somehow to the truth about these matters?

d PRO.: We certainly must.

SOC.: Come on, then. Here is a further point we need to agree on.

PRO.: What is that?

SOC.: That each of us will be trying to prove some possession or state of the soul to be the one that can render life happy for all human beings.[2] Isn't that so?   └ *the human good is a state of the soul*

PRO.: Quite so.

SOC.: You, that it is pleasure; we, that it is knowledge?

PRO.: That is so.

SOC.: What if it should turn out that there is another possession, better *e* than either of them? Would the result not be that, if it turns out to be more closely related to pleasure, we will both lose out against a life *12* that firmly possesses that, but the life of pleasure will defeat the life of knowledge?

PRO.: Yes.

SOC.: And if it is closer to knowledge, then knowledge wins over pleasure, and pleasure loses? Do you accept this as agreed?[3]

PRO.: It seems agreeable to me.

SOC.: But also to Philebus? Philebus, what do you say?

PHI.: To my mind pleasure wins and always will win, no matter what.[4] But you must see for yourself, Protarchus.

---

1. One of the results of the dialogue is a differentiation among the intellectual capacities (cf. 55c ff; 66b–c).

2. The context shows that pleasure and knowledge are not mere instrumental goods but *constitute* happiness.

3. Socrates' third possibility anticipates the dialogue's result (66a–c). Why it might be the right solution is first discussed at 22a–b.

4. Most of Philebus' scanty remarks show him as an unreformable hedonist. His replacement by a more open-minded spokesman shows that Plato has abandoned the combative form of dialogue.

PRO.: But now you have handed over the argument to us, Philebus, you can no longer control the agreements we make with Socrates nor our disagreements.

PHI.: You are right. I absolve myself of all responsibility and now call the *b* goddess herself as my witness.

PRO.: We will be your witnesses, too,—that you did say what you are now saying. As to what follows, Socrates, let us go ahead and try to push through to a conclusion, with Philebus' consent or not.

SOC.: We must do our best, making our start with the goddess herself— this fellow claims that though she is called Aphrodite her truest name is pleasure.

PRO.: Certainly.

SOC.: I always feel a more than human dread over what names to use for *c* the gods—it surpasses the greatest fear.[1] So now I address Aphrodite by whatever title pleases her.[2] But as to pleasure, I know that it is complex and, just as I said, we must make it our starting point and consider carefully what sort of nature it has. If one just goes by the name it is one single thing, but in fact it comes in many forms that are in some way even quite unlike each other. Think about it: we say that a debauched person gets pleasure, as well as that a sober-minded person takes pleasure in his very *d* ˣ sobriety. Again, we say that a fool, though full of foolish opinions and hopes, gets pleasure, but likewise a wise man takes pleasure in his wisdom.[3] But surely anyone who said in either case that these pleasures are like one another would rightly be regarded as a fool.

PRO.: Well, yes, Socrates—the pleasures come from opposite things. But *they* are not at all opposed to one another. For how could pleasure not be, of all things, most like pleasure? How could that thing not be most like *e* itself?

SOC.: Just as color is most like color! Really, you surprise me: Colors certainly won't differ insofar as every one of them is a color; but we all know that black is not only different from white but is in fact its very opposite. And shape is most like shape in the same way. For shape is all

---

1. Socrates' fear is explained in *Cratylus* 400d–401a: We don't know anything about the gods' names but can at best study human beliefs manifested in the names we give them.

2. The gods, as perfect beings, are not subject to pleasure and pain, as will soon emerge (33b), and Aphrodite turns out to prefer law and order over unlimited pleasure (26b–c). That it is an insult to the goddess to call lust "aphrodisiac" is indicated also in the *Seventh Letter* (335b).

3. On the difference between foolish and wise pleasures cf. 40a–c; 63d–e.

13   one in genus, but some of its parts are absolutely opposite to one another, and others differ in innumerable ways.[1] And we will discover many other such cases. So don't rely on this argument which makes a unity of all the things that are most opposed. I am afraid we will find there are some pleasures that are contrary to others.

PRO.: Maybe so. But how will this harm our thesis?

SOC.: Because you call these unlike things, we will say, by a different name. For you say that all pleasant things are *good*. Now, no one contends

b   that pleasant things are not pleasant. But while most of them are bad but some good, as we hold, you nevertheless call them all good, even though you would admit that they are unlike one another if someone pressed the point. What is the common element in the good and bad pleasures that allows you to call them all good?

PRO.: What are you saying, Socrates? Do you think anyone will agree to this who begins by laying it down that pleasure is the good? Do you think

c   he will accept it when you say that some pleasures are good but others are bad?[2]

SOC.: But you will grant that they are *unlike* each other and that some are opposites?

PRO.: Not insofar as they are pleasures.

SOC.: But really, Protarchus, this takes us back to the same old point. Are we, then, to say that pleasure does not differ from pleasure, but all are alike? Don't the examples just given make the slightest impression on us? Are we to behave and speak in just the same way as those who are the

d   most incompetent and at the same time newcomers in such discussions?

PRO.: What way do you mean?

SOC.: This: Suppose I imitate you and dare to say, in defense of my thesis, that the most unlike thing is of all things most *like* the most unlike; then I could say the same thing as you did.[3] But this would make us look quite childish, and our discussion would founder on the rock. Let us therefore

1. The decision of the question whether pleasure is a genus with different species and opposite qualities is of the greatest importance for the dialogue. When his analogies don't convince Protarchus, Socrates resorts to a rather desperate appeal: The possibility of further discussion depends on it (13c–d; 14a).

2. Protarchus is clever enough to avoid Socrates' trap. So far he has not admitted that pleasures are unlike each other, let alone that there are good and bad ones.

3. The fallacy works if *being unlike* is treated as a regular predicate. Such tricks were used in sophistic debates, and Plato lets old Parmenides use the device he calls childish here in *Prm.* 147c–148b.

set it afloat again. Perhaps we can reach mutual accommodation if each side accepts a similar stance toward its candidate.

PRO.: Just tell me how.   *e*

SOC.: Let me be the one questioned in turn by you.

PRO.: About what?

SOC.: About wisdom, knowledge, understanding, and all the things that I laid down at the beginning as good, when I tried to answer the question what is good. Won't my answer suffer the same consequences as your thesis did?

PRO.: How so?

SOC.: Taken all together, the branches of knowledge will seem to be a plurality, and some will seem quite unlike others. And if some of them turn out in some way actually to be opposites, would I be a worthy partner *14* in a discussion if I dreaded this so much that I would deny that one kind of knowledge can be unlike another? That way our whole discussion would come to an end like that of a fairy tale—with us kept safe and sound through some absurdity.[1]

PRO.: We must not let that happen, except the part about our being kept safe and sound. But I am rather pleased by the fact that our theses are on the same footing. So let it be agreed that there can be many and unlike kinds of pleasures, but also many and different kinds of knowledge. *λ*

SOC.: Well, then, let us not cover up the difference between your good *b* and mine, Protarchus, but put it right in the middle and brave the possibility that, when put to a closer scrutiny, it will come to light whether pleasure should be called the good, or wisdom, or yet a third thing. For we are not contending here out of love of victory for my suggestion to win or for yours. We ought to act together as allies in support of the truest one.

PRO.: We certainly ought to.

II. The "dialectical" part of the investigation: the classification of pleasure and knowledge (14b–31b)

1. The problem of the One and Many (14b–20a)

SOC.: Let us then give even stronger support to our principle by an *c* agreement.

---

1. It is not clear whether Plato is merely referring to unmotivated turns in fairy tales in general, or perhaps to the attainment of a happy end through the pronouncement of some magic words.

PRO.: What principle?

SOC.: The one that creates difficulties for everyone, for some willingly, for some, sometimes, against their will.

PRO.: Explain this more clearly.

SOC.: It is this principle that has turned up here, which somehow has an amazing nature. For that the many are one and the one many are amazing statements, and can easily be disputed, whichever side of the two one may want to defend.

PRO.: Do you mean this in the sense that someone says that I, Protarchus, *d* am one by nature but then also says that there are many 'me's' and even contrary ones, when he treats me, who am one and the same, as tall and short, heavy and light, and endless other such things?

SOC.: You, dear Protarchus, are speaking about those puzzles about the one and many that have become commonplace. They are agreed by everybody, so to speak, to be no longer even worth touching; they are considered childish and trivial but a serious impediment to argument if one takes *e* them on.[1] No more worthy is the following quibble: when someone who first distinguishes a person's limbs and parts asks your agreement that all these parts are identical with that unity, but then exposes you to ridicule because of the monstrosities you have to admit, that the one is many and indefinitely many, and again that the many are only one thing.

PRO.: But what other kinds of such puzzles with respect to the same principle do you have in mind, Socrates, that have not yet admittedly become commonplace?

15 SOC.: When, my young friend, the *one* is not taken from the things that come to be or perish, as we have just done in our example. For that is where the sort of one belongs that we were just discussing, which we agreed is not worthy of scrutiny. But when someone tries to posit man as one, or ox as one, or the beautiful as one, and the good as one, zealous concern with divisions of these unities and the like gives rise to controversy.

PRO.: In what sense?

b SOC.: Firstly, whether one ought to suppose that there are any such unities truly in existence. Then again, how they are supposed to be: whether each one of them is always one and the same, admitting neither of generation nor of destruction; and whether it remains most definitely one and the

---

1. The problem of individual unity and plurality was taken seriously in *Phd.* 101, *R.* 523c–525a and *Sph.* 251a–c. In *Prm.*129c, it is treated as a pseudo-problem. Here attention is drawn to the fact that they are concerned with the unity and plurality of genus and species, not with individual things and their properties.

same, even though it is afterwards found again among the things that come to be and are unlimited, so that it finds itself as one and the same in one and many things at the same time.* And must it be treated as dispersed and multiplied or as entirely separated from itself, which would seem most impossible of all? It is these problems of the one and many, but not those others, Protarchus, that cause all sorts of difficulties if they are not properly settled, but promise progress if they are.   *c*

PRO.: Is this the first task we should try our hands at right now, Socrates?

SOC.: So I would say at least.

PRO.: Take it, then, that we all here are agreed with you about this. As for Philebus, it might be best not to bother him with questions any further, but let sleeping dogs lie.

SOC.: Quite so. Now, where should we make our entry into that complex   *d* and wide-ranging battle about this controversial issue? Is it not best to start here?

PRO.: Where?

SOC.: By making the point that it is through *discourse* that the same thing flits around, becoming one and many in all sorts of ways, in whatever it may be that is said at any time, both long ago and now. And this will never come to an end, nor has it just begun, but it seems to me that this is an "immortal and ageless" condition[1] that comes to us with discourse. Whoever among the young first gets a taste of it is as pleased as if he had found   *e* a treasure of wisdom. He is quite beside himself with pleasure and revels in moving every statement, now turning it to one side and rolling it all up into one, then again unrolling it and dividing it up. He thereby involves first and foremost himself in confusion, but then also whatever others happen to be nearby, be they younger or older or of the same age, sparing neither his father nor his mother nor anyone else who might listen to him.   *16* He would almost try it on other creatures, not only on human beings, since he would certainly not spare any foreigner if only he could find an interpreter somewhere.[2]

1. Socrates uses the customary epithet of the gods (cf. Homer, *Il.* viii.539) to show how serious the problem is. The ambiguity of language, whether words have a unitary and unchangeable meaning, is a serious problem with a flip side that is exploited by the boys who make fun of it.

2. This description of the exploitation of the problem by naughty boys recalls strikingly (even in the words used) Socrates' explanation why boys should not have access to dialectic

* The punctuation is that of Diès, on the assumption that there are two rather than three problems addressed. This problem is discussed in the Introductory Essay (cf. xxi–xxii).

PRO.: Careful, Socrates, don't you see what a crowd we are and that we are all young? And are you not afraid that we will gang up against you with Philebus if you insult us?[1] Still, we know what you want to say, and if there are some ways and means to remove this kind of disturbance from our
b discussion in a peaceful way, and to show us a better solution to the problem, then just go ahead, and we will follow you as best we can. For the present question is no mean thing, Socrates.

SOC.: It certainly is not, my boys, as Philebus is wont to address you. Indeed, there is not, nor could there be, any way that is finer than the one
χ I have always admired, although it has often escaped me and left me behind, alone and helpless.

PRO.: What is this way? Let us have it.

c SOC.: It is not very difficult to describe it, but extremely difficult to use. For everything in any field of art that has ever been discovered has come to light because of this. See what way I have in mind.

PRO.: Please do tell us.

So.: It is a gift of the gods to men, or so it seems to me, hurled down from heaven by some Prometheus along with a most dazzling fire.[2] And the people of old, superior to us and living in closer proximity to the gods,
d have bequeathed us this tale, that/whatever is said to be consists of one and many, having in its nature limit and unlimitedness. Since this is the structure of things, we have to assume that there is in each case always one form for every one of them, and we must search for it, as we will indeed find it there. And once we have grasped it, we must look for two, as the case would have it, or if not, for three or some other number. And we must treat every one of those further unities in the same way, until it is not only established of the original unit that it is one, many and unlimited,

---

(*R.* 539b). The image there is of a dog tearing around and shredding things to pieces, while here Socrates seems to be thinking of the spreading out or rolling together of dough (or perhaps wool). Cf. also the remarks on the feasts for young boys and late-learners in *Sph.* 252a–c.

1. This echoes Phaedrus' threat to Socrates (*Phdr.* 236c–d). Plato seems to be suggesting that the Socrates here is indeed the old Socrates.

2. The 'Prometheus' here is generally identified as Pythagoras. The crucial pair of terms, 'limit' and 'unlimited' (*peras* and *apeiron*), plays an important role in Pythagoreanism, as the report in Aristotle (*Met.* A 986a15–b5, cf. the commentary of W.D. Ross, vol. I 148–152) shows clearly. But the Pythagoreans applied these terms most of all to numbers themselves. The use Plato intends to make of that pair in his dialectical method of *collection* and *division* is rather different. Nevertheless, Plato is justified in describing the Pythagorean innovation as a flash of enlightenment. Where there had been chaos, there was now an orderly multitude, so that scientific thinking and methodical investigation could begin.

but also how many kinds it is.[1] For we must not grant the form of the unlimited to the plurality before we know the exact number of every plurality that lies between the unlimited and the one. Only then is it permitted to release each kind of unity into the unlimited and let it go. The gods, as I said, have left us this legacy of how to inquire and learn and teach one another. But nowadays the clever ones among us make a one, haphazardly, and a many, faster or slower than they should; they go straight from the one to the unlimited and omit the intermediates. It is these, however, that make all the difference as to whether we are engaged with each other in dialectical or only in eristic discourse.[2]

PRO.: Some of what you said I think I understand in some way, Socrates, but of some I still need further clarification.

SOC.: What I mean is clear in the case of letters, and you should take your clue from them, since they were part of your own education.

PRO.: How so?

SOC.: The sound that comes out of the mouth is one for each and every one of us, but then it is also unlimited in number.

PRO.: No doubt.

SOC.: Neither of these two facts alone yet makes us knowledgeable, neither that we know its unlimitedness nor its unity. But if we know how many kinds of vocal sounds there are and what their nature is, that makes every one of us literate.[3]

1. The method of collection of the items in a given field by establishing the unity of the highest genus and dividing the members into subgenera, species, and subspecies was part of the training in dialectic in Plato's Academy. The schema of division is discussed in *Phdr.* 265a–266b. Demonstrations of divisions are found in *Sph.* (esp. 218b–231c; 264b–268d) and the *Statesman* (258b–268d). Plato is more rigorous in his demand for numerical accuracy in *Phlb.* than elsewhere, but he also stresses the need for economy in the numbers of divisions in *Plt.* 287c.

2. Vagueness and ambiguity of language constituted the basic capital of the sophists' business. Most fallacies can be avoided if the expressions used are properly defined; Plato hopes to achieve this with the dialectical method.

3. Letters and also notes in music constitute Plato's favorite illustrations of basic elements in nature, cf. *Sph.* 253a–c, *Ti.* 48b–c; *Tht.* 202d–206b. The model of how writing is taught is also used to demonstrate the conditions of learning and its deficiencies elsewhere: *Euthd.* 277a; *R.* 402a–b, *Cra.* 431e–432a; *Plt.* 277e–278d; *Tht.* 163b–c, 207d–208b. It is problematic whether by "letters" Plato here means the phonemes or the written character. Ryle, although he admits that Plato might have conflated the two, has argued forcefully for the phonemes (1960), but serious objections have been raised against his interpretation by Gallop, who points out that Plato had good reason to treat letters and their sounds together (1963). This explains why Plato passes without hesitation from the voice to the characters.

PRO.: Very true.

SOC.: And the very same thing leads to the knowledge of music.

PRO.: How is that?

c SOC.: Sound is also the unit in this art, just as it was in writing.

PRO.: Yes, right.

SOC.: We should posit low and high pitch as two kinds, and equal pitch as a third kind. Or what would you say?

PRO.: Just that.

SOC.: But you could not yet claim knowledge of music if you knew only this much, though if you were ignorant even about that, you would be quite incompetent in these matters, as one might say.

PRO.: Certainly.

SOC.: But you will be competent, my friend, once you have learned how many intervals there are in high pitch and low pitch, what character they

d have, by what notes the intervals are defined, and the kinds of combinations they form—all of which our forebears have discovered and left to us, their successors, together with the names of these modes of harmony.[1] And again the motions of the body display other and similar characteristics of this kind, which they say should be measured by numbers and called rhythms and meters.[2] So at the same time they have made us realize that every investigation should search for the one and many. For when you

e have mastered these things in this way, then you have acquired expertise there, and when you have grasped the unity of any of the other things there are, you have become wise about that.[3] The boundless multitude, however, in any and every kind of subject leaves you in boundless igno-

1. It is much more difficult in music than in the case of letters to see how the method of division could work to identify all sounds, since the division of sounds into high, low, and even does not seem adequate to provide a scheme for the identification of the sounds. For an attempt to "save" the example and to accommodate the complex set of musical modes cf. Introd. p. xxvi–xxviii.

2. Socrates can explain rhythm by reference to body movements because music was intimately connected with dance. So the division into long and short measures ("feet") had a quite literal sense; the lengths and shortnesses were not abstract time units. The difficulties of performing division in metrics is similar to that in music; apart from the division into long and short measures combinations of units will have to be taken into consideration.

3. The crucial point in the discussion of the 'divine method' is that Plato proposes a *holistic* model of knowledge. There cannot be knowledge of any items in isolation; to know what *one* letter is we have to know the whole field of *grammata* and their interconnections. This has important consequences for our understanding of Plato's theory of Forms, as it is to be found in the *Phlb*. For it urges that Forms cannot be known in isolation either, but only in relation to one another. For a discussion of the "field-concept of knowledge", cf. G. Fine (1979) and D. Frede (1989).

rance, and makes you count for nothing and amount to nothing, since you have never worked out the amount and number of anything at all.

PRO.: For my part, I think that Socrates has explained all this very well, Philebus.

PHI.: I agree as far as this question itself goes. But of what use is all this *18* talk to us, and what is its purpose?

SOC.: Philebus is right, Protarchus, when he asks us this question.

PRO.: Good, so please answer him.

SOC.: I will do so when I have gone a little further into the subject matter. Just as someone who has got hold of some unity or other should not, as we were saying, immediately look for the unlimited kind but first look for some number, so the same holds for the reverse case. For if he is forced to start out with the unlimited, then he should not head straight for the one, but should in each case grasp some number that determines every *b* plurality whatever, and from all of those finally reach the one. Let us again make use of letters to explain what this means.

PRO.: In what way?

SOC.: The way some god or god-inspired man discovered that vocal sound is unlimited, as tradition in Egypt claims for a certain deity called Theuth.[1] He was the first to discover that the vowels in that unlimited variety are not one but several, and again that there are others that are not voiced, *c* but make some kind of noise, and that they, too, have a number.[2] As a third kind of letters he established the ones we now call mute. After this he further subdivided the ones without sound or mutes down to every single unit. In the same fashion he also dealt with the vowels and the intermediates, until he had found out the number for each one of them, and then he gave all of them together the name "letter." And as he realized

1. The Egyptian god of writing is also cited in *Phdr.* 274c–275b as the inventor of the art of writing (as well as of most other intellectual disciplines, including the games of draughts and dice). Theuth's invention is there criticized by King Thamus because the art of writing weakens rather than strengthens people's memory and knowledge. Memory and true understanding will suffer because of their reliance on written records that are open to everyone. This charming story explains Plato's reservations against writing and his preference for the living speech of which the written is only an image (276a).

2. It has been objected that Theuth's procedure is not a proper example of proceeding "bottom up" from the unlimited to generic unity (cf. Hackforth (1945), 25–26), because Theuth has the notion of a generic unity all along. But Theuth, though aiming at generic unity, proceeds towards it from the unlimited multitude through the collection of intermediary unities (vowels, consonants, and semiconsonants). No one can practice dialectic without knowing both of collection and division, but knowing the schema does not determine the particular procedure or direction.

that none of us could gain any knowledge of a single one of them,
d taken by itself without understanding them all, he considered that
the one link that somehow unifies them all and called it the art of
literacy.[1]

PHI.: Protarchus, I understood this even better than what came before, at
least how it hangs together. But I still find that this explanation now suffers
from the same defect as your earlier one.

SOC.: You are wondering again what the relevance of it all is, Philebus?

PHI.: Right, that is what I and Protarchus have been wanting to see for
quite a while.

SOC.: But have you not already under your nose what you both, as you
e say, have long wanted to see?

PHI.: How could that be?

SOC.: Did we not embark on an investigation of knowledge and pleasure,
to find out which of the two is preferable?

PHI.: Yes, indeed.

SOC.: And we do say that each of them is one.

PHI.: Right.

SOC.: This is the very point in question to which our preceding
discussion obliges us to give an answer: to show how each of them
19 is one and many, and how instead of becoming unlimited straightaway,
each one of them acquires some definite number before it becomes
unlimited.

PRO.: Socrates has plunged us into a considerable problem, Philebus, by
leading us around, I don't know how, in some kind of circle. But make up
your mind which of us should answer the present question. It would seem
quite ridiculous that I, who had volunteered to take over the thesis from
you as your successor, should now hand it back to you because I don't
have an answer to this question. But it would be even more ridiculous if
b neither of us could answer it. So what do you think we should do? Socrates
seems to be asking whether there are *kinds* of pleasures or not, and how
many there are, and of what sort they are. And the same set of questions
applies to knowledge.

SOC.: You speak the truth, son of Callias. Unless we are able to do this
for every kind of unity, similarity, sameness, and their opposite, in the way

---

1. On Plato and the Egyptian alphabet, cf. Eisler (1922). How much Plato knew about
Egypt, whether he visited it, is a much debated question. Phaedrus accuses Socrates of
inventing the story of Theuth, and Socrates admits as much (*Phdr.* 275b), but this does not
mean that Plato could not have had firsthand experience of Egyptian culture.

that our recent discussion has indicated, none of us will ever turn out to be any good at anything.[1]

PRO.: I am afraid that this is so. But while it is a great thing for the *c* wise man to know everything, the second best is not to be mistaken about oneself, it seems to me.[2] What prompts me to say that at this point? I will tell you. You, Socrates, have granted this meeting to all of us, and yourself to boot, in order to find out what is the best of all human possessions. Now, Philebus advocated that it is pleasure, amusement, enjoyment, and whatever else there is of this kind. You on the contrary denied this for all of them, but rather proposed those *d* other goods we willingly and with good reason keep reminding ourselves of, so that they can be tested as they are lying side by side in our memory. You claim, it seems, that the good that should by right be called superior to pleasure, at least, is reason, as well as knowledge, intelligence, science, and everything that is akin to them, which must be obtained, rather than Philebus' candidates. Now, after both these conflicting positions have been set up against each other, we threatened *e* you in jest that we would not let you go home before the deliberation of these questions had reached its satisfactory limit. But since you made a promise and committed yourself to us, we therefore insist, like children, that there is no taking back a gift properly given. So give up this way of turning against us in the discussion here.

SOC.: What way are you talking about?

PRO.: Your way of plunging us into difficulties and repeating questions *20* to which we have at present no proper answer to give you. But we should not take it that the aim of our meeting is universal confusion; if we cannot solve the problem, you must do it, for you promised. It is up to you to decide whether for this purpose you need to divide off different kinds of pleasure and knowledge or can leave that out, if you are able and willing to show some other way to settle to issues of our controversy.

---

1. The enumeration of the general terms unity, similarity, sameness, and their opposites (i.e. plurality, dissimilarity, and difference) shows that Socrates is here referring to competence in dialectic.

2. Protarchus is here stating his version of the Delphic demand of self-knowledge. He realizes he is not up to the task, either of performing the divisions or of finding some other means, and therefore he asks Socrates to fulfill his promise to find a way out of their difficulties. These are the longest pronouncements Protarchus makes in the dialogue, and he thereby surrenders the guidance of the discussion to Socrates as the virtual advocate for both sides.

2. The Dream of Socrates and the compromise solution (20b–23b)

b Soc.: At least there is no longer anything terrible in store for poor me, since you said it this way. For the clause "if you are willing" takes away all further apprehension. In addition, some memory has come to my mind that one of the gods seems to have sent me to help us.[1]

Pro.: How is that and what about?

Soc.: It is a doctrine that once upon a time I heard in a dream—or perhaps I was awake—that I remember now, concerning pleasure and knowledge, that neither of the two is the good, but that there is some third thing which

c is different from and superior to both of them. But if we can clearly conceive now that this is the case, then pleasure has lost its bid for victory. For the good could no longer turn out to be identical with it. Right?

Pro.: Right.

Soc.: So we will not have to worry any longer, I think, about the division of kinds of pleasure. But further progress will show this more clearly.

Pro.: Very well said; just push on.

Soc.: There are some small matters we ought to agree on first, though.

Pro.: What are they?

d Soc.: Whether the good is necessarily bound to be perfect or not perfect.

Pro.: But surely it must be the most perfect thing of all, Socrates!

Soc.: Further: must the good be sufficient?[2]

Pro.: How could it fail to be that? This is how it is superior to everything else there is.

Soc.: Now, this point, I take it, is most necessary to assert of the good: that everything that has any notion of it hunts for it and desires to get hold of it and secure it for its very own, caring nothing for anything else except for what is connected with the acquisition of some good.

Pro.: There is no way of denying this.

e Soc.: So let us put the life of pleasure and the life of knowledge on trial, and reach some verdict by looking at them separately.

1. In spite of the fact that Socrates clearly knows where he is going, there is a lot about divine inspiration in this dialogue. Apart from the "gift of the gods" at 16c5, referred to again as the source of their theory at 23c9, there is the prayer for divine assistance at 25b–c, and there is yet another such prayer for the final mixture at 61b. Plato uses this device not only to justify a change in direction, such as the sudden dumping of the burden of division, but also when he lets Socrates propose un-Socratic suggestions, such as the three criteria adopted as tests for the good life. Socrates' sudden "dream" refers to his early surmise of a third possibility at 11e.

2. Perfection and sufficiency might look like the same thing, but perfection stresses that no further additions are possible, sufficiency that nothing is lacking.

PRO.: In what way do you mean?

SOC.: Let there be neither any knowledge in a life of pleasure, nor any pleasure in that of knowledge. For if either of the two is the good, then it must have no need of anything in addition. But if one or the other should turn out to be lacking anything, then this can definitely no longer be the *21* real good we are looking for.

PRO.: How could it be?

SOC.: So shall we then use *you* as our test case to try both of them?

PRO.: By all means.

SOC.: Then answer me.

PRO.: Go ahead.

SOC.: Would you find it acceptable to live your whole life in enjoyment of the greatest pleasures?

PRO.: Why, certainly!

SOC.: And would you see yourself in need of anything else if you had secured this altogether?

PRO.: In no way.

SOC.: But look, might you not have some need of knowledge, intelligence, and calculation, or anything else that is related to them?*   *b*

PRO.: How so? If I had pleasure I would have all in all!

SOC.: And living like that you could enjoy the greatest pleasures through-out your life?

PRO.: Why should I not?

SOC.: Since you would not be in possession of either reason, memory, knowledge, or true opinion, must you not be in ignorance, first of all, about this very question, whether you were enjoying yourself or not, given that you were devoid of any kind of intelligence?[1]

PRO.: Necessarily.

SOC.: Moreover, due to lack of memory, it would be impossible for you to   *c* remember that you ever enjoyed yourself, and for any pleasure to survive from one moment to the next, since it would leave no memory. But, not possessing right judgment, you would not realize that you are enjoying your-self even while you do, and, being unable to calculate, you could not figure

---

1. On the question whether it is fair to 'subtract' any recognition of enjoyment from pleasure cf. Introd. p. xxxii. In the *Ti.* Plato ascribes awareness but no *doxa* of pleasure and pain to plants (77b *aisthesis*), so his separation of pleasure and understanding here is not an ad hoc device against hedonism.

* Deleting *ta deonta*, following Badham and Diès.

out any future pleasures for yourself. You would thus not live a human life but the life of a mollusk or of one of those creatures in shells that live in the

d sea.[1] Is this what would happen, or can we think of any other consequences besides these?

PRO.: How could we?

SOC.: But is this a life worth choosing?

PRO.: Socrates, this argument has left me absolutely speechless for the moment.[2]

SOC.: Even so, let us not give in to weakness; let us in turn rather inspect the life of reason.

PRO.: What kind of life do you have in mind?

SOC.: Whether any one of us would choose to live in possession of every kind of intelligence, reason, knowledge, and memory of all things, while

e having no part, neither large nor small, of pleasure or of pain, living in total insensitivity of anything of that kind.

PRO.: To me at least neither of these two forms of life seems worthy of choice, nor would it to anyone else, I presume.[3]

22 SOC.: But what about a combination of both, Protarchus, a life that results from a mixture of the two?

PRO.: You mean a mixture of pleasure with reason and intelligence?

SOC.: Right, those are the ingredients I mean.

PRO.: Everybody would certainly prefer this life to either of the other two, without exception.[4]

SOC.: Do we realize what the upshot of this new development in our discussion is?

PRO.: Certainly, that of the three lives offered to us, two are not sufficient

b or worthy of choice for either man or animal.

SOC.: As far as they are concerned, is it then not clear at least, that neither

---

1. That the uncompromising hedonist lives a low type of life (a steady influx and flowing out is discussed already in the *Grg.* (492e–494b), where Socrates compares it with that of a duck. Here he chooses an even lower type of animal.

2. This is the dialogue's only *elenchus*, properly so called. The only other point where Protarchus has given in, the plurality of pleasure, was conceded not through force of argument but by appeal.

3. In the *Grg.* Socrates regards the pleasureless life as preferable, in spite of the fact that Callicles calls it the life of a stone (492e, 494a–b). That his readiness to compromise in *Phlb.* is only a partial change of mind on Plato's part will emerge later.

4. Protarchus is portrayed as completely forgetful of his friend Philebus' position that he so recently shared. Plato seems intent on showing how complete a conversion to Socrates' view the *elenchus* has achieved.

the one nor the other contained the good, since otherwise it would be sufficient, perfect, and worthy of choice for any of the plants and animals that can sustain them, throughout their lifetime? And if anyone among us should choose otherwise, then he would do so involuntarily, in opposition to what is by nature truly choiceworthy, from ignorance or some unfortunate necessity.[1]

PRO.: It certainly looks that way.

SOC.: Enough has been said, it seems to me, to prove that Philebus'   *c*
goddess and the good cannot be regarded as one.

PHI.: Nor is your reason the good, Socrates, and the same complaint applies to it.

SOC.: It may apply to *my* reason, Philebus, but certainly not to the true, the divine reason, I should think. It is in quite a different condition.[2] But now I am not arguing that reason ought to get first prize over and against the combined life; we have rather to look and make up our minds about   *d*
the second prize, how to dispose of it. One of us may want to give credit for the combined life to reason, making it responsible, the other to pleasure. Thus neither of the two would be the good, but it could be assumed that one or the other of them is its *cause*.[3] But I would be even more ready to contend against Philebus that, whatever the ingredient in the mixed life may be that makes it choiceworthy and good, reason is more closely related to that thing and more like it than pleasure; and if this can   *e*
be upheld, neither first nor second prize could really ever be claimed for pleasure. She will in fact not even get as much as third prize, if we can put some trust in my insight for now.[4]

PRO.: By now it seems to me indeed that pleasure has been defeated as if knocked down by your present arguments, Socrates. In her fight for victory, she has fallen. And as for reason, we may say that it wisely did not   *23*
compete for first prize, for it would have suffered the same fate. But if pleasure were also deprived of second prize, she would definitely be somewhat dishonored in the eyes of her own lovers, nor would she seem as fair to them as before.

1. We will meet such an unfortunate person in 44b–e.

2. Socrates indicates here that his concessions about reason and knowledge are limited to *human* reason. This is an important fact to be kept in mind for the evaluation of the dialogue's overall result. On the difference between divine and human reason cf. 28c ff. Divine and human reason are also contrasted in *Phdr.* 247c–d; 278d; *Prm.* 134c–e.

3. This function of being the cause will soon be assigned to reason, although it will not be the most important determining factor in the good either (28b–30e; 66b).

4. Pleasure actually will get only the fifth and last rank on the scale of goods (66c).

SOC.: What, then? Had we not better leave her alone now, rather than subject her to the most exacting test and give her pain by such an examination?

PRO.: You talk nonsense, Socrates.

b SOC.: Why, because I said the impossible, "giving pain to pleasure"?

PRO.: Not only that, but because you don't realize that not one among us would let you go before you have carried the discussion of these questions to its end.[1]

3. The fourfold division of all beings (23c–27c)

SOC.: Oh, dear, Protarchus, then a long discussion lies ahead of us, and not exactly an easy one either at this point. For it seems that, in the battle about the second prize for reason, a different device will be needed, different armament as it were, from that used in our previous discussion, though it may partly be the same.[2] Are we to proceed?

PRO.: Of course.

c SOC.: Let us be very careful about the starting point we take.

PRO.: What kind of starting point?

SOC.: Let us make a division of everything that actually exists now[3] in the universe into two kinds, or if this seems preferable, into three.

PRO.: Could you explain on what principle?

SOC.: By taking up some of what has been said before.

PRO.: Like what?

SOC.: We agreed earlier that the god had revealed a division of what is into the unlimited and the limit.

PRO.: Certainly.

---

1. Note should be taken of the humorous tone, which is more subdued than in many earlier dialogues, but persists through most of the discussion.

2. For a discussion of the problem in what sense the "armament" is partially the same cf. Introd. p. xxxvii–viii. I take it that what constitutes the partial identity is not the rather different use of *limit* and *unlimited*, but the (rudimentary) application of *division* and *collection*.

3. The interpretation of the "now" is problematic. Some interpreters take it to indicate that only the sensible objects in the universe fall under the fourfold division, so that the Forms are excluded (cf. Hackforth (1945), 37–43, who dismisses various authors' efforts to find a place for the Forms). A different possibility, advocated here, is that the "now" emphasizes the all-inclusiveness of this division, as opposed to the earlier application of the dialectical method, which dealt with the highest genera of particular disciplines. If all genera and species are Forms, there will be Forms as well as sensibles in all four kinds. This is the interpretation suggested in Striker's monograph.

Soc.: Let us now take these as two of the kinds, while treating the one that results from the mixture of these two as our third kind. But I must look like quite a fool with my distinctions into kinds and enumerations! *d*

Pro.: What are you driving at?

Soc.: That we seem to be in need of yet a fourth kind.

Pro.: Tell us what it is.

Soc.: Look at the cause of this combination of those two together, and posit it as my fourth kind in addition to those three.

Pro.: Might you not also be in need of a fifth kind that provides for their separation?[1]

Soc.: Perhaps, but I do not think so, at least for now. But if it turns out that I need it, I gather you will bear with me if I should search for a fifth kind. *e*

Pro.: Gladly.

Soc.: Let us first take up three of the four, and since we observe that of two of them, both are split up and dispersed into many, let's make an effort to collect them into a unity again, in order to study how each of them is in fact one and many.

Pro.: If you could explain all that more clearly, I might be able to follow you.

Soc.: What I mean is this: The two kinds are the ones I referred to just now, the unlimited and what has limit.[2] That the unlimited in a way is many I will try to explain now. The treatment of what has limit will have to wait a little longer. *24*

Pro.: Let it wait.

Soc.: Attention, then. The matter I am asking you to attend to is difficult and controversial, but attend to it nevertheless. Check first in the case of the hotter and the colder whether you can conceive of a limit, or whether the 'more and less' do not rather reside in these kinds, and while they reside in them do not permit the attainment of any end.[3] For once an end has been reached, they will both have been ended as well. *b*

---

1. The causes of separation, as the discussion of pleasure and pain will show (31b ff.), are not uniform, but include whatever may cause decay of a mixture.

2. Whether and in what sense this new sense of *peras* and *apeiron* constitutes the missing link to the 'esoteric Plato' is discussed in Introd. §4. Plato wavers between calling the limit just "limit" and "what has limit". Since the limit consists of a measure or proportion of the ingredients of a mixture, the expression "what has limit" may refer to the fact that the measure imposes or constitutes limit.

3. At first it seems as if only relative terms make up the class of the unlimited. But later Plato adds nonrelatives such as the high and low, the fast and the slow, frost and heat (26a)

PRO.: Very true.

SOC.: We are agreed, then, that the hotter and the colder always contain the more and less.

PRO.: Quite definitely.

SOC.: Our argument forces us to conclude that these things never have an end. And since they are endless, they turn out to be entirely unlimited.

PRO.: Quite strongly so, Socrates.

SOC.: You have grasped this rather well, Protarchus, and remind me rightly
c with your pronouncement of 'strongly' that it and equally its counterpart 'gently' are of the same caliber as the more and less. Wherever they apply, they prevent everything from adopting a definite quantity; by imposing on all actions the qualification 'stronger' relative to 'gentler' or the reverse, they procure a 'more and less' while doing away with all definite quantity. We are saying now, in effect, that if they do not abolish definite quantity, but let quantity and measurement take a foothold in the domain of the
d more and less, the strong and mild, they will be driven out of their own territory. For once they take on a definite quantity, they would no longer be hotter and colder. The hotter and equally the colder are always in flux and never remain, while definite quantity means standstill and the end of all progression. The upshot of this argument is that the hotter, together with its opposite, turn out to be unlimited.[1]

PRO.: That seems to be its result, Socrates, although, as you said yourself, it is difficult to follow in these matters. But if they are repeated again and
e again, perhaps both questioner and respondent may end up in a satisfactory state of agreement.

SOC.: A good idea; let us carry it out. But consider whether, to avoid the needless length of going through a complete survey of all cases, the following indication may serve to mark out the nature of the unlimited.

PRO.: What indication do you have in mind?

---

to it. This has led to the conclusion that *Phlb.* must predate the *Plt.* (283a–e), where the two cases are carefully distinguished, cf. Waterfield (1980). But this conclusion seems wrong. Plato has no reason to introduce distinctions that are not relevant and here would only confuse the philosophically untrained Protarchus. Both the hot and the hotter are unlimited because these qualities do not contain any quantities, therefore they both permit the more and less (cf. Introd. xxxiii ff.).

1. These qualifications might seem to assign all entities with a definite degree to the mixed class. It will become clear, however, that only *harmonious* mixtures belong there, so we have to assume that any quality that is not 'just right' is unlimited. It is not only always relative to some other item because there is no ideal standard, but also possibly in eternal flux since nothing keeps it stable.

Soc.: Whatever seems to us to become 'more and less', or susceptible to 'strong and mild' or to 'too much' and all of that kind, all that we ought to subsume under the genus of the unlimited as its unity. This is in compliance with the principle we agreed on before, that for whatever is dispersed and split up into a multitude, we must try to work out its unifying nature as far as we can, if you remember.

Pro.: I do remember.

Soc.: But look now at what does not admit of these qualifications but rather their opposites, first of all 'the equal' and 'equality' and, after the equal, things like 'double', and all that is related as number to number or measure to measure: If we subsume all these together under the heading of 'limit', we would seem to do a fair job.[1] Or what do you say?

Pro.: A very fair job, Socrates.

Soc.: Very well, then. But what nature shall we ascribe to the third kind, the one that is the mixture of the two?

Pro.: You will have to answer that question for me, I think.

Soc.: A god rather, if any of them should listen to my prayers.

Pro.: So say your prayer, and wait for the result.

Soc.: I am waiting, and indeed I have the feeling that one of the gods is favorably disposed to us now, Protarchus.

Pro.: What do you mean by that, and what evidence have you?

Soc.: I certainly will tell you, but you follow closely what I say.

Pro.: Just go on.

Soc.: We called something hotter and colder just now, didn't we?

Pro.: Yes.

Soc.: Now add dryer and wetter to them, and more and less, faster and slower, taller and shorter, and whatever else we have previously collected together as the one kind that has the nature of taking on the 'more and less'.

Pro.: You mean the nature of the unlimited?

Soc.: Yes. Now take the next step and mix with it the class of the limit.

Pro.: Which one?

Soc.: The very one we have so far omitted to collect together, the class that has the character of limit, although we ought to have given unity to it, just as we collected together the unlimited kind. But perhaps it will

---

1. There is a problem about the exact determination of limit here: Are only numbers and magnitudes limits that can stand in relation to other numbers and magnitudes as their equal or double, or are the equal and the double themselves limits? I plead for the former interpretation with Striker (1979), 58–61.

come to the same thing even now if, through the collection of these two kinds, the unity of the former kind becomes conspicuous too.[1]

PRO.: What kind do you mean, and how is this supposed to work?

SOC.: The kind that contains equal and double, and whatever else puts an end to the conflicts there are among opposites, making them commensurate and harmonious by imposing a definite number on them.

PRO.: I understand. I have the impression that you are saying that, from such mixture in each case, certain generations result?

SOC.: Your impression is correct.

PRO.: Then go on with your explanation.

SOC.: Is it not true that in sickness the right combination of the opposites establishes the state of health?[2]

26 PRO.: Certainly.

SOC.: And does not the same happen in the case of the high and the low, the fast and the slow, which belong to the unlimited? Is it not the presence of these factors in them* which forges a limit and thereby creates the different kinds of music in their perfection?[3]

PRO.: Beautiful!

SOC.: And once engendered in frost and heat, limit takes away their excesses and unlimitedness, and establishes moderation and harmony in that domain?

PRO.: Quite.

b SOC.: And when the unlimited and what has limit are mixed together, we are blessed with seasons and all sorts of fine things of that kind?

PRO.: Who could doubt it?

SOC.: And there are countless other things I have to pass by in silence: With health there come beauty and strength, and again in our soul there is a host of other excellent qualities. It is the goddess herself, fair Philebus,

---

1. Although limit has been identified with numbers and magnitudes, it now becomes clear that not just any kind of number or proportion is a limit. The omission for which Socrates blames himself is due to the fact that the selection of such numbers depends on the mixture in question, so the unity of the genus cannot be established a priori.

2. The right combination of opposites is the right amount of the hot and cold, the dry and the wet.

3. The example confirms my claim that not any limit makes a mixture. The question where music is concerned is not that only a definite degree puts a stop to eternally sliding sounds, but that it is the mixture of the right notes that makes for music; the same applies to rhythm. For a physical explanation cf. *Ti.* 80a–b.

---

* Retaining *eggignomena* in the text at 26a3, leaving out the colon after *tauta*.

who recognizes how excess and the overabundance of our wickedness
allow for no limit in our pleasures and their fulfilment, and she therefore
imposes law and order as a limit on them.[1] And while you may complain
that this ruins them, I by contrast call it their salvation. How does this
strike you, Protarchus?

PRO.: This fits my own intuitions, Socrates.

SOC.: These, then, are the three kinds I spoke of, if you see what I mean.

PRO.: I think I've got it. It seems to me that you are referring to the
unlimited as one kind, to the limit within things as the other, second kind.
But I still do not sufficiently understand what you mean by the third.

SOC.: You are simply overwhelmed by the abundance of the third kind,
my admirable friend. Although the class of the unlimited also displays a
multiplicity, it preserved at least the appearance of unity, since it was
marked out by the common character of the more and less.

PRO.: That is true.

SOC.: About limit, on the other hand, we did not trouble ourselves,*
neither that it has plurality nor whether it is one by nature.[2]

PRO.: Why should we have done so?

SOC.: No reason. But see what I mean by the third kind: I treat all the
joint offspring of the other two kinds as a unity, a coming-into-being
created through the measures imposed by the limit.[3]

PRO.: I understand.

1. The goddess must be Aphrodite herself (*pace* Hackforth, l.c. 48n3), because it is she who
puts a curb on pleasure, thereby saving it. Socrates had already expressed reservations about
identifying pleasure and the goddess (b–c), but now it is clear that she has deserted Philebus'
case just as Protarchus has. In the *Smp.* two Aphrodites were distinguished, a heavenly and
a vulgar one (180c–181a), and the *Phdr.* has much to say about the limits of love (253c ff.).

2. No attempt had been made to identify the kinds of limits there are, nor what common
character unites the numbers and magnitudes that constitute limits. To determine this would
presuppose a discussion of the good on a cosmic level, a question that is not addressed in
the dialogue.

3. The extension of the third kind has been debated. Since Plato is very explicit that
harmonious mixtures are at stake when he discusses reason as their only possible efficient
cause and selects appropriate candidates (health, beauty, strength, virtues of the soul, 26b)
no other mixtures seem feasible. In addition, he later says that without measure there is no
mixture, but only an "unconnected medley" (64e). For the question of what to make of
"coming-into-being", cf. Introd. p. lviin3. As the later association of pleasure with *genesis*
and the end product with *being* suggests (54c), the 'being' assigned to successful mixtures
should not be played down.

* Adopting Bury's insertion of *hoti* before *polla* at d4.

e Soc.: But now we have to look at the fourth kind we mentioned earlier, in addition to these three. Let this be our joint investigation. See now whether you think it necessary that everything that comes to be comes to be through some cause?

Pro.: Certainly, as far as I can see. How could anything come to be without one?

Soc.: And is it not the case that there is no difference between the nature of what *makes* and the *cause*, except in name, so that the maker and the cause would rightly be called one?

Pro.: Right.

27 Soc.: But what about what is made and what comes into being, will we not find the same situation, that they also do not differ except in name?

Pro.: Exactly.

Soc.: And isn't it the case that what makes is always leading in the order of nature, while the thing made follows since it comes into being through it?

Pro.: Right.

Soc.: Therefore the cause and what is subservient to the cause in a process of coming-into-being are also different and not the same?

Pro.: How should they be?

Soc.: It follows, then, that what comes to be and that from which it is produced represent all three kinds?[1]

Pro.: Very true.

b Soc.: We therefore declare that the craftsman who produces all these must be the fourth kind, the cause, since it has been demonstrated sufficiently that it differs from the others?[2]

Pro.: It certainly is different.

Soc.: Now that the four kinds have been distinguished, it seems right to go through them one by one, for memory's sake.

Pro.: Of course.

Soc.: As the first I count the unlimited, limit as the second, afterwards in third place comes the being which is mixed and generated out of those

c two. And no mistake is made if the cause of this mixture and generation is counted as number four?

Pro.: How could there be one?

---

1. I.e. the mixture and its two ingredients, limit and the unlimited.

2. The use of the word *demiourgos* here seems a deliberate reference to the demiurge in *Ti.* 41a. The ensuing macrocosm-microcosm argument confirms this. All order comes from a rational source.

4. The genera of pleasure and knowledge (27c–31b)

SOC.: Now, let's see, what is going to be our next point after this, and what concern of ours got us to this point? Was it not this? We were wondering whether second prize should be awarded to pleasure or to knowledge, wasn't that it?

PRO.: It was indeed.

SOC.: On the basis of our fourfold distinction we may now perhaps be in a better position to come to a decision about the first and the second prize, the issue that started our whole debate.

PRO.: Perhaps.

SOC.: Let us continue, then. We declared the life that combines pleasure   *d*
and knowledge the winner.[1] Didn't we?

PRO.: We did.

SOC.: Should we not take a look at this life and see what it is and to which kind it belongs?

PRO.: Nothing to prevent us.

SOC.: We will, I think, assign it to the third kind,[2] for it is not a mixture of just two elements but of the sort where all that is unlimited is tied down by limit.* It would seem right, then, to make our victorious form of life part of that kind.

PRO.: Very right.

SOC.: That is settled, then. But how about your kind of life, Philebus,   *e*
which is pleasant and unmixed? To which of the established kinds should it by right be assigned? But before you make your pronouncement, answer me the following question.

PHI.: Just tell me!

SOC.: Do pleasure and pain have a limit, or are they of the sort that admit the more and less?

PHI.: Certainly the sort that admit the more, Socrates! For how could pleasure be all that is good if it were not by nature boundless in plenty and increase?

SOC.: Nor would, on the other hand, pain be all that is bad, Philebus! So   *28*

---

1. In the final ranking the mixed life obtains only second prize (66b).
2. That the good life should be a harmonious mixture does not need much of a justification. Pleasure is one of its unlimited ingredients, but here Socrates indicates that it contains more unlimited elements, which must be in the right proportion.

---

* Reading *mikton ekeino* with Schütz and Diès.

we have to search for something besides its unlimited character that would
bestow on pleasures a share of the good. But take note that pleasure* is
thereby assigned to the boundless. As to assigning intelligence, knowledge,
and reason to one of our aforesaid kinds, how can we avoid the danger of
blasphemy, Protarchus and Philebus? A lot seems to hinge on whether or
not we give the right answer to this question.

b PHI.: Really now, you are extolling your own god, Socrates.[1]

SOC.: Just as you extoll that goddess of yours, Philebus. But the question
needs an answer, nevertheless.

PRO.: Socrates is right in this, Philebus; we must obey him.

PHI.: Didn't you choose to speak instead of me?

PRO.: Quite. But now I am at a loss, and I entreat you, Socrates, to act as
our spokesman, so that we do not misstate the case of your candidate and
thus introduce a false note into the discussion.

c SOC.: Your obedient servant, Protarchus, especially since it is not a very
difficult task. But did my playful exaltation really confuse you, as Philebus
claims, when I asked to what kind reason and knowledge belonged?

PRO.: It certainly did, Socrates.[2]

SOC.: It is easy to settle, nevertheless. For all the wise are agreed, in true
self-exaltation, that reason is our king, both over heaven and earth.[3] And
perhaps they are justified. But let us go into the discussion of this class
itself at greater length, if you have no objections.

d PRO.: Discuss it in whichever way you like, Socrates, and don't be apolo-
getic about longwindedness; we will not lose patience.

SOC.: Well said. Let us proceed by taking up this question.

PRO.: What question?

1. Philebus is angry because Socrates has elevated the misclassification of his candidate to
sacrilege, thereby deifying reason.

2. Protarchus (without the benefit of the *Timaeus*) is puzzled because he does not yet see
what possible sacrilege there could be.

3. *Zeus basileus* (Zeus as king) of traditional religion is here replaced by *nous basileus*, reason
as king. But Zeus will soon be reinstalled and identified with the cosmic *nous* (30d). Plato
is exaggerating when he claims agreement of all thinkers, but many pre-Socratics did assume
some sort of rational principle as the cause maintaining the order of the universe, among
them Xenophanes, Heraclitus, and Anaxagoras. I can see no reason here for distinguishing
between an immanent and a transcendent reason (cf. Hackforth et al., l.c. 56n1). The
following argument establishes in a roundabout way that cosmic reason does all the things
it is credited with.

* Accepting the correction of *touto* with Ven. 189 and Diès.

Soc.: Whether we hold the view that the universe and this whole world order are ruled by unreason and irregularity, as chance would have it, or whether they are not rather, as our forebears taught us, governed by reason and by the order of a wonderful intelligence.

Pro.: How can you even think of a comparison here, Socrates? What you   *e* suggest now is downright impious, I would say. The only account that can do justice to the wonderful spectacle presented by the cosmic order of sun, moon, and stars and the revolution of the whole heaven, is that reason arranges it all, and I for my part would never waver in saying or believing it.[1]

Soc.: Is this what you want us to do, that we should not only conform to the view of earlier thinkers who professed this as the truth, repeating   *29* without any risk what others have said, but that we should share their risk and blame if some formidable opponent denies it and argues that disorder rules?

Pro.: How could I fail to want it?

Soc.: Well, then, now face up to the consequences of this position that we have to come to terms with.

Pro.: Please tell me.

Soc.: We somehow discern that what makes up the nature of the bodies of all animals—fire, water, air, "and earth!", as storm-battered sailors say[2]—are part of their composition.

Pro.: Very much so. We are indeed battered by difficulties in our dis-   *b* cussion.

Soc.: Come, now, and realize that the following applies to all constituents that belong to us.

Pro.: What is it?

Soc.: That the amount of each of these elements in us is small and insignificant, that it does not possess in the very least the purity or the power that is worthy of its nature. Take one example as an illustration representative for all. There is something called fire that belongs to us, and then again there is fire in the universe.

Pro.: No doubt.

Soc.: And is not the fire that belongs to us small in amount, feeble and   *c*

1. This is a remarkable pronouncement in the mouth of a disciple of Gorgias (58a). Socrates' warning, that one should not just adopt conventional wisdom but "share [its] risk," shows that he is not convinced of the well-foundedness of Protarchus' enthusiasm.

2. The pun cannot be imitated, because English-speaking sailors would sigh for "land", not "earth". For such a welcome cf. Aeschylus, *Agamemnon* 899.

poor, while the fire in the universe overwhelms us by its size and beauty and by the display of all its power?

PRO.: What you say is very true.

SOC.: But what about this? Is the fire in the universe generated, nourished, and ruled by the fire that belongs to us, or is it not quite the reverse, that your heat and mine, and that in every animal, owe all this to the cosmic fire?

PRO.: It is not even worth answering that question.

d SOC.: Right. And I guess you will give the same answer about the earth here in the animals when it is compared to earth in the universe, and likewise about the other elements I mentioned a little earlier. Is that your answer?

PRO.: Who could answer differently without seeming insane?

SOC.: No one at all. But now see what follows. To the combination of all these elements taken as a unit we give the name "body", don't we?

PRO.: Certainly.

e SOC.: Now, realize that the same holds in the case of what we call the ordered universe. It will turn out to be a body in the same sense, since it is composed of the same elements.

PRO.: What you say is undeniable.

SOC.: Does the body of the universe as a whole provide for the sustenance of what is body in our sphere, or is it the reverse, and the universe possesses and derives all the goods enumerated from ours?

PRO.: That too is a question not worth asking, Socrates.

30 SOC.: But what about the following, is this also a question not worth asking?

PRO.: Tell me what the question is.

SOC.: Of the body that belongs to us, will we not say that it has a soul?

PRO.: Quite obviously that is what we will say.

SOC.: But where does it come from, unless the body of the universe which has the same properties as ours, but more beautiful in all respects, happens to possess a soul?

PRO.: Clearly from nowhere else.

SOC.: We surely cannot maintain this assumption, with respect to our four

b classes (limit, the unlimited, their mixture, and their cause—which is present in everything): that this cause is recognized as all-encompassing wisdom, since among us it imports the soul[1] and provides training for the

---

1. Since it seems wrong to say that reason *gives* (*parechon*) the soul to the body, as the mss have it, but orders it (cf. 28e2) and maintains it, it would be preferable to read something like "*katechon*" (= "possess", "master", cf. *archein* 30d4; 64b4 and *Ti.* 37c3). Although 30c9

body and medicine for its ailments and in other cases order and restitution, but that it should fail to be responsible for the same things on a large scale in the whole universe (things that are, in addition, beautiful and pure),[1] for the contrivance of what has so fair and wonderful a nature.

PRO.: That would make no sense at all. *c*

SOC.: But if that is inconceivable, we had better pursue the alternative account and affirm, as we have said often, that there is plenty of the unlimited in the universe as well as sufficient limit, and that there is, above them, a certain cause, of no small significance, that orders and coordinates the years, seasons, and months, and which has every right to the title of wisdom and reason.

PRO.: The greatest right.

SOC.: But there could be no wisdom and reason without a soul.

PRO.: Certainly not.

SOC.: You will therefore say that in the nature of Zeus there is the soul *d* of a king, as well as a king's reason, in virtue of this power displayed by the cause, while paying tribute for other fine qualities in the other divinities, in conformity with the names by which they like to be addressed.[2]

PRO.: Very much so.

SOC.: Do not think that we have engaged in an idle discussion here, Protarchus, for it comes as a support for the thinkers of old who held the view that reason is forever the ruler over the universe.

PRO.: It certainly does.

SOC.: It also has provided an answer to my query, that reason belongs to that kind which is the cause of everything.[3] But that was one of our four *e* kinds. So there you already have the solution to our problem in your hands.

PRO.: I have indeed, and quite to my satisfaction, although at first I did not realize that you were answering.

SOC.: Sometimes joking is a relief from seriousness.

PRO.: Well said.

---

confirms soul as a necessary condition for reason and wisdom, the point here is that reason *establishes* order in the soul, just as it does in the body.

1. Plato must be referring to the world soul here, its ordering and governance by cosmic reason.

2. On the different character traits represented by the gods, cf. *Phdr.* 252c–253c.

3. The reason why and in what sense Plato established his macrocosm-microcosm parallel should be clear by now. It is in fact not a mere parallel or analogy, for human reason can cause a harmonious mixture only because of its derivation from divine reason. As such it grasps the *principle* of limit to be imposed on the unlimited.

31 Soc.: By now, dear friend, we have arrived at a satisfactory explanation of the class that reason belongs to and what power it has.
Pro.: Quite so.
Soc.: And as to pleasure, it became apparent quite a while ago what class it belongs to.
Pro.: Definitely.
Soc.: Let us firmly keep it in mind about both of them, that reason is akin to cause and is part of that family, while pleasure itself is unlimited and belongs to the kind that in and by itself neither possesses nor will ever possess a beginning, middle, or end.[1]
b Pro.: We will keep it in mind, how could we help it?

III. The "critical" part of the investigation: critique of pleasure and knowledge (31b–59d)

1. The critique of pleasure: the nature of pleasure and pain (31b–36c)

Soc.: After this we must next find out in what kind of thing each of them resides and what kind of condition makes them come to be when they do. Let us take pleasure first, for just as we searched for the class it belongs to first, so we start our present investigation with it. But again, we will not be able to provide a satisfactory examination of pleasure if we do not study it together with pain.
Pro.: If that is the direction we have to take, then let's go that way.
Soc.: Do you share my view about their generation?
c Pro.: What view?
Soc.: Pleasure and pain seem to me by nature to arise together in the common kind.[2]

---

1. This sums up the importance of the results of the dialectical part of the argument for the critique of pleasure and knowledge. The nature of the genus of each of them determines the flaws they may have.

2. After determining their *genus*, Socrates now *locates* pleasure and pain. They are not independent phenomena, but occur in things that represent a harmonious mixture. They are now first identified with the natural *restoration* and unnatural *disintegration* of the harmonious state of limit and unlimitedness (32b); subsequently some necessary qualifications will be made to that simple model. That health is a state of natural balance or equilibrium was a common presupposition in Greek medicine; it was shared by many pre-Socratic philosophers as well. For Plato, it will emerge, the 'medical' point of view applies to all pleasures.

PRO.: Could you remind us once again, Socrates, which of those you mentioned you called the common kind?[1]

SOC.: As far as I can, my most esteemed friend.

PRO.: That is noble of you.

SOC.: By the common kind, we meant the one that was number three on our list of four.

PRO.: You mean the one you introduced after the unlimited and the limited, the one that included health, and also harmony, I believe?

SOC.: Excellently stated. But now try to put your mind to this as much as *d* possible.

PRO.: Just go on.

SOC.: What I claim is that when we find the harmony in living creatures disrupted, there will at the same time be a disintegration of their nature and a rise of pain.

PRO.: What you say is very plausible.

SOC.: But if the reverse happens, harmony is regained and the former nature restored, we have to say that pleasure arises, if we must pronounce only a few words on the weightiest matters in the shortest possible time.

PRO.: I believe that you are right, Socrates, but why don't we try to be *e* more explicit about this very point?

SOC.: Well, is it not child's play to understand the most ordinary and well-known cases?

PRO.: What cases do you mean?

SOC.: Hunger, I take it, is a case of disintegration and pain?

PRO.: Yes.

SOC.: And eating, the corresponding refilling, is a pleasure?

PRO.: Yes.

SOC.: But thirst is, once again, a destruction and pain, while the process that fills what is dried out with liquid is pleasure? And, further, unnatural *32* separation and dissolution, the affection caused by heat, is pain, while the natural restoration of cooling down is pleasure?

PRO.: Very much so.

SOC.: And the unnatural coagulation of the fluids in an animal through freezing is pain, while the natural process of their dissolution or redistribution is pleasure. To cut matters short, see whether the following account seems acceptable to you. When the natural combination of limit and *b* unlimitedness that forms a live organism, as I explained before, is de-

---

1. The repetitions indicate not only that Protarchus is not much used to such debates, but that the distinction itself is a novel one.

stroyed, this destruction is pain, while the return towards its own nature, this general restoration, is pleasure.

PRO.: So be it, for it seems to provide at least an outline.

SOC.: Shall we then accept this as one kind of pleasure and pain, what happens in either of these two kinds of processes?

PRO.: Accepted.

SOC.: But now accept also the anticipation by the *soul* itself of these two
c kinds of experiences; the hope before the actual pleasure will be pleasant and comforting, while the expectation of pain will be frightening and painful.

PRO.: This turns out then to be a different kind of pleasure and pain, namely the *expectation* that the soul experiences by itself, without the body.

SOC.: Your assumption is correct. In both these cases, as I see it at least, pleasure and pain will arise pure and unmixed with each other, so that it will become apparent as far as pleasure is concerned whether its whole
d class is to be welcomed or whether this should rather be the privilege of one of the other classes which we have already discussed.[1] Pleasure and pain may rather turn out to share the predicament of hot and cold and other such things that are welcome at one point but unwelcome at another, because they are not good, but it happens that some of them do occasionally assume a beneficial nature.

PRO.: You are quite right if you suggest that this must be the direction to take if we want to find a solution to what we are looking for now.

SOC.: First, then, let us take a look together at the following point. If it
e truly holds, as we said, that their disintegration constitutes pain, but restoration is pleasure, what kind of state should we ascribe to animals when they are neither destroyed nor restored; what kind of condition is this? Think about it carefully, and tell me: Is there not every necessity that the animal will at that time experience neither pain nor pleasure, neither large nor small?

PRO.: That is indeed necessary.

SOC.: There is, then, such a condition, a third one, besides the one in
33 which one is pleased or in which one is in pain?

PRO.: Obviously.

SOC.: Make an effort to keep this fact in mind. For it makes quite a difference for our judgment of pleasure whether we remember that there

---

1. Where the body is involved, pleasure and pain are inextricably intertwined, because the pleasure of eating is not to be had without the pain of hunger. In the case of the soul's anticipations, there is allegedly no such admixture of the opposite state.

is such a state or not.[1] But we had better give it a little more consideration, if you don't mind.

PRO.: Just tell me how.

SOC.: You realize that nothing prevents the person who has chosen the life of reason from living in this state.

PRO.: You mean without pleasure and pain? *b*

SOC.: It was one of the conditions agreed on in our comparison of lives that the person who chooses the life of reason and intelligence must not enjoy pleasures either large or small.

PRO.: That was indeed agreed on.

SOC.: He may then live in this fashion, and perhaps there would be nothing absurd if this life turns out to be the most godlike.

PRO.: It is at any rate not likely that the gods experience either pleasure or the opposite.

SOC.: It is certainly not likely. For either of these states would be quite unseemly in their case. But this is a question we had better take up again later if it should be relevant to our discussion, but let us count it as an *c* additional point in favor of reason in the competition for second prize, even if we cannot count it in that for first prize.[2]

PRO.: A very good suggestion.

SOC.: But now as for the other kind of pleasure, of which we said that it belongs to the soul itself. It depends entirely on memory.

PRO.: In what way?

SOC.: It seems we have first to determine what kind of a thing memory is; in fact I am afraid that we will have to determine the nature of perception even before that of memory, if the whole subject matter is to become at all clear to us in the right way.

PRO.: How do you mean? *d*

SOC.: You must realize that some of the various affections of the body are extinguished within the body before they reach the soul, leaving it unaffected. Others penetrate through both body and soul and provoke a kind of upheaval that is peculiar to each but also common to both of them.[3]

---

1. This third state can be no other than a state of health and harmony, but Socrates does not yet make it quite clear that the pleasureless and painless state of reason *is* such a state of perfect harmony.

2. The paradox that the most godlike state is not the best one attainable for human beings will be dissolved only gradually: Our needy nature does not permit us to live that way.

3. There is no strict separation of pleasures of soul and body; the latter always involve the soul as well. Processes unnoticed by the soul are not pleasures or pains. But mere *awareness* is not sufficient to explain even the most simple 'physical' pains like hunger. They involve

PRO.: I realize that.

SOC.: Are we fully justified if we claim that the soul remains oblivious of those affections that do not penetrate both, while it is not oblivious of those that penetrate both?

e PRO.: Of course we are justified.

SOC.: But you must not so misunderstand me as to suppose I meant that this 'obliviousness' gave rise to any kind of forgetting.[1] Forgetting is rather the loss of memory, but in the case in question here no memory has yet arisen. It would be absurd to say that there could be the process of losing something that neither is nor was in existence, wouldn't it?

PRO.: Quite definitely.

SOC.: You only have to make some change in names, then.

PRO.: How so?

SOC.: Instead of saying that the soul is oblivious when it remains unaffected by the disturbances of the body, now change the name of what you so far

34 called obliviousness to that of *nonperception*.

PRO.: I understand.

SOC.: But when the soul and body are jointly affected and moved by one and the same affection, if you call this motion *perception*, you would say nothing out of the way.

PRO.: You are right.

SOC.: And so we know by now what we mean by perception?

PRO.: Certainly.

SOC.: So if someone were to call memory the 'preservation of perception', he would be speaking correctly, as far as I am concerned.

b PRO.: Rightly so.

SOC.: And do we not hold that recollection differs from memory?

PRO.: Perhaps.

SOC.: Does not their difference lie in this?

PRO.: In what?

SOC.: Do we not call it 'recollection' when the soul recalls as much as possible by itself, without the aid of the body, what she

---

functions of the soul besides perception, *viz.* memory and desire. That Plato is so painstakingly slow here shows that this analysis of pleasure and pain is new. In *Tht.* 156b and *Ti.* 64a–65b they are still subsumed under sense-perception.

1. In Greek there is an etymological relation between *lanthanein* (escape notice) and *lethe* (forgetting); the point can be made in English if we recall the original meaning of the Latin root of "oblivious".

had once experienced together with the body?[1] Or how would you put it?

PRO.: I quite agree.

SOC.: But on the other hand, when, after the loss of memory of either a perception or again of a piece of knowledge, the soul calls up this memory   *c* for itself, we also call all these events recollection.

PRO.: You are right.

SOC.: The point for the sake of which all this has been said is the following.

PRO.: What is it?

SOC.: That we grasp as fully and clearly as possible the pleasure that the soul experiences without the body, as well as the desire. And through a clarification of these states, the nature of both pleasure and desire will somehow be revealed.[2]

PRO.: Let us now discuss this as our next issue, Socrates.

SOC.: It seems that in our investigation we have to discuss many points   *d* about the origin of pleasure and about all its different varieties. For it looks as if we will first have to determine what desire is and on what occasion it arises.

PRO.: Let us determine that, then. We have nothing to lose.

SOC.: We will certainly lose something, Protarchus; by discovering what we are looking for now, we will lose our ignorance about it.

PRO.: You rightly remind us of that fact. But now let us try to return to the further pursuit of our subject.

SOC.: Are we agreed now that hunger and thirst and many other things of this sort are desires?   *e*

PRO.: Quite in agreement.

SOC.: But what is the common feature whose recognition allows us to address all these phenomena, which differ so much, by the same name?

PRO.: Heavens, that is perhaps not an easy thing to determine, Socrates, but it must be done nevertheless.

SOC.: Shall we go back to the same point of departure?

PRO.: What point?

---

1. "Recollection" here means merely the retrieval of an experience in the past in *this* life. There is no question of *anamnesis* of a former life. The careful dissection of the different functions are meant to help separate the different kinds of pleasures from their contributing factors.

2. Desire is not a pleasurelike state, as Plato used to think (cf. his pairing off *hedone kai epithumia*, *Grg.* 484d, *R.* 328d, *Phdr.* 273d), nor is it identical with the anticipation of a pleasure. It rather turns out to be a pain of the soul, conditioned by the dissolution of the body and the memory of its restitutions.

SOC.: When we say "he is thirsty," we always have something in mind?
PRO.: We do.
SOC.: Meaning that he is getting empty?
PRO.: Certainly.
SOC.: But thirst is a desire?
PRO.: Yes, the desire for drink.
35 SOC.: For drink or for the filling with drink?
PRO.: For the filling with drink, I think.
SOC.: Whoever among us is emptied, it seems, desires the opposite of what he suffers. Being emptied, he desires to be filled.
PRO.: That is perfectly obvious.
SOC.: But what about this problem? If someone is emptied for the first time, is there any way he could be in touch with filling, either through sensation or memory, since he has no experience of it, either in the present or ever in the past?
PRO.: How should he?
b SOC.: But we do maintain that he who has a desire desires something?
PRO.: Naturally.
SOC.: He does, then, not have a desire for what he in fact experiences. For he is thirsty, and this is a process of emptying. His desire is rather of filling.
PRO.: Yes.
X SOC.: Something in the person who is thirsty must necessarily somehow be in contact with filling.
PRO.: Necessarily.
SOC.: But it is impossible that this should be the body, for the body is what is emptied out.
PRO.: Yes.
SOC.: The only option we are left with is that the soul makes contact with
c the filling, and it clearly must do so through memory. Or could it make contact through anything else?
PRO.: Clearly through nothing else.
SOC.: Do we understand, then, what conclusions we have to draw from what has been said?
PRO.: What are they?
SOC.: Our argument forces us to conclude that desire is not a matter of the body.
PRO.: Why is that?
SOC.: Because it shows that every living creature always strives towards the opposite of its own experience.

PRO.: And very much so.

SOC.: This impulse, then, that drives it towards the opposite of its own state signifies that it has memory of that opposite state?

PRO.: Certainly.

SOC.: By pointing out that it is this memory that directs it towards the *d* objects of its desires, our argument has established that every impulse, desire, and the rule over the whole animal is the domain of the soul.[1]

PRO.: Very much so.

SOC.: Our argument will, then, never allow that it is our body that experiences thirst, hunger, or anything of that sort.

PRO.: Absolutely not.

SOC.: There is yet a further point we have to consider that is connected with these same conditions. For our discussion seems to me to indicate that there is a form of life that consists of these conditions.

PRO.: What does it consist of, and what form of life are you talking about? *e*

SOC.: It consists of filling and emptying and all such processes as are related to both the preservation and the destruction of animals. And when one of us is in either of the two conditions, he is in pain, or again he experiences pleasure, depending on the nature of these changes.[2]

PRO.: That is indeed what happens.

SOC.: But what if someone finds himself in between these two affections?

PRO.: What do you mean by "in between"?

SOC.: When he is pained by his condition and remembers the pleasant things that would put an end to the pain, but is not yet being filled. What about this situation? Should we claim that he is then in between these two *36* affections, or not?

PRO.: We should claim that.

SOC.: And should we say that the person is altogether in pain or pleasure?

PRO.: By heaven, he seems to me to be suffering a twofold pain; one consists in the body's condition, the other in the soul's desire caused by the expectation.

---

1. So desire is a pain based on the memory of the requisite state of fulfillment. The point of this careful analysis of the different factors is to establish that pains and pleasures are *intentional* (object-directed) states, since all involve memory, except for the negligible case of the newborn that has no memory and therefore no desire but only pain. The unravelling of the many factors involved will provide the basis for the critique of pleasure.

2. This "way of life" is our normal condition; it cannot be good as such, because it inevitably involves pain. Socrates focuses here on the moment "between" pain and pleasure in order to analyze the influence of our *expectations* in that situation. (The "in between" is, of course, not to be confused with the neutral, third state of neither pleasure nor pain.)

Soc.: How do you mean that there is a twofold pain, Protarchus? Does it not sometimes happen that one of us is emptied at one particular time,
b but is in clear hope of being filled, while at another time he is, on the contrary, without hope?

Pro.: It certainly happens.

Soc.: And don't you think that he enjoys this hope for replenishment when he remembers, while he is simultaneously in pain because he has been emptied at that time?

Pro.: Necessarily.

Soc.: This is, then, the occasion when a human being and other animals are simultaneously undergoing pain and pleasure.

Pro.: It seems so.

Soc.: But what if he is without hope of attaining any replenishment when he is emptied? Is not that the situation where this twofold pain occurs,
c which you have just come across and simply taken to be twofold?[1]

Pro.: That is quite undeniable, Socrates.

2. The question of false pleasures (36c–50e)

Soc.: Now let us apply the results of our investigation of these affections to this purpose.

Pro.: What is it?

Soc.: Shall we say that these pains and pleasures are true or false, or rather that some of them are true, but not others?

Pro.: But how could there be false pleasures or pains, Socrates?

Soc.: Well, how could there be true or false fears, true or false expectations, true or false judgments, Protarchus?[2]

d Pro.: For judgments I certainly would be ready to admit it, but not for the other cases.

---

1. This completes the separation of pleasures and pains of body and soul. Although no pleasure is a matter of the body alone, the pleasure of expectation or the pain of hopelessness belong to the soul alone, even if their *occasion* is provided by the joint condition of soul and body. This answers the question at 32b–c, whether we would find expectations pleasant when not in need: We would not, but the expectation itself is a matter of the soul alone. In that it differs from desire.

2. In spite of his careful preparations for these pleasures of the soul alone, Socrates has an uphill fight to prove that they can be true and false in the same sense as judgments. It will turn out that certain pleasures are themselves judgments.

SOC.: What is that you are saying? I am afraid we are stirring up a weighty controversy here.

PRO.: You are right.

SOC.: But if it is relevant to what we were discussing before, you worthy son of that man, it ought to be taken up.

PRO.: Perhaps, in that case.

SOC.: We have to forego any excursions here or any discussion of whatever side issues are not directly relevant to our topic.[1]

PRO.: Right.

SOC.: But tell me this, for I have lived in continued perplexity about the   *e* difficulty we have come across now. What is your view? Are there not false pleasures, as well as true ones?

PRO.: How should there be?

SOC.: Do you really want to claim that there is no one who, either in a dream or awake, either in madness or any other delusion, sometimes believes he is enjoying himself, while in reality he is not doing so, or believes he is in pain while he is not?

PRO.: We all assume that this is indeed the case, Socrates.

SOC.: But rightly so? Should we not rather take up the question whether or not this claim is justified?[2]

PRO.: We should take it up, as I at least would say.

SOC.: Let us try to achieve more clarity about what we said concerning   *37* pleasure and judgment. Is there something we call judging?

PRO.: Yes.

SOC.: And is there also taking pleasure?

PRO.: Yes.

SOC.: But there is also what the judgment is about?

PRO.: Certainly.

---

1. Plato thereby indicates that the long discussion of false pleasures is not an excursion but directly relevant to their task.

2. Socrates is not going to overturn this conviction; the subsequent discussion rather works out in what sense it is justified (cf. 40d). The "facticity" of pleasure is granted immediately (although later the possibility will be discussed of confusing freedom from pain with pleasure, 43d ff.). Now the question is whether there can nevertheless be something wrong with pleasure. Plato is not only out to correct the hedonist, he is also straightening out unclarities in his own earlier treatment of pleasure. In *R.* IX, his only extensive earlier discussion of pleasure and pain, he questions the reality of all but the philosopher's pleasures (583b–587a). The most important innovation in *Phlb.* is the establishment of a literal truth and falsity of pleasures that have propositional content.

Soc.: And also what the pleasure is about? *i.e., the object of pleasure*
Pro.: Very much so.
Soc.: But what makes a judgment, whether it judges rightly or not, cannot
be deprived of really making a judgment.
b Pro.: How should it?
Soc.: And what takes pleasure, whether it is rightly pleased or not, can
obviously never be deprived of really taking pleasure.
Pro.: Yes, that is also the case.
Soc.: But what we have to question is how it is that judgment is usually
either true or false, while pleasure admits only truth, even though in both
cases there is equally real judgment and real pleasure.[1]
Pro.: We have to question that.
Soc.: Is it that judgment takes on the additional qualification of true and
c false and is thus not simply judgment, but also has either one of these two
qualities? Would you say that is a point we have to look into?
Pro.: Yes.
Soc.: And furthermore, whether quite generally certain things allow extra
qualifications, while pleasure and pain are simply what they are and do
not take on any qualifications. About that we also have to come to an
agreement.
Pro.: Obviously.
Soc.: But at least it is not difficult to see that they, too, take on qualifications. For we said earlier that both of them, pleasures as well as pains, can
be great and small, and also have intensity.
d Pro.: We certainly did.
Soc.: But if some bad state should attach itself to any of them, then we
would say that the judgment becomes a bad one, and the pleasure becomes
bad too, Protarchus?
Pro.: Naturally, Socrates.
Soc.: But what if some rightness or the opposite of rightness are added
to something, would we not call the judgment right, if it were right, and
the pleasure too?
Pro.: Necessarily.
e Soc.: And if a mistake is made about the object of judgment, then we say

---

1. The question of further qualifications for pleasure had been in dispute at the beginning
of the dialogue (12c ff.). It led to the discussion of unity and plurality. Now the question of
goodness and badness is replaced by that of truth and falsity. Socrates is very careful here:
He paves the way via some qualifications that have already been admitted, namely that
pleasures have size.

that the judgment that makes that mistake is not right and does not judge rightly?

PRO.: How could it?

SOC.: But what if we notice that a pain or pleasure is mistaken in what it is pleased or pained about, shall we then call it right or proper or give it other names of praise?

PRO.: That would be impossible, if indeed pleasure should be mistaken.

SOC.: As to pleasure, it certainly often seems to arise in us not with a right, but with a false, judgment.

PRO.: Of course. But what we call false in this case at that point is the 38 judgment, Socrates; nobody would dream of calling the pleasure itself false.[1]

SOC.: You certainly put up a spirited defense for pleasure now, Protarchus!

PRO.: Not at all; I only repeat what I hear.

SOC.: Is there no difference between the pleasure that goes with right judgment and knowledge and the kind that often comes to any of us with false judgment and ignorance?

PRO.: There's probably no small difference. *b*

SOC.: So let us turn to inspect the difference between them.

PRO.: Lead on where you like.

SOC.: I lead you this way.

PRO.: What way?

SOC.: Of our judgment we say that it is sometimes false, and sometimes true?

PRO.: It is.

SOC.: And as we said just now, these are often accompanied by pleasure and pain. I am talking of true and false judgment.

PRO.: That's right.

SOC.: And is it not memory and perception that lead to judgment or the attempt to come to a definite judgment, as the case may be?

PRO.: Indeed. *c*

SOC.: Do we agree that the following must happen here?

PRO.: What?

---

1. At first Socrates' attempt to establish truth and falsity by analogy with judgment misfires. Protarchus separates what is judgmental about pleasure (its content) from the pleasure itself. So he has not given up his 'epiphenomenal' view that pleasure, the feeling, is separable from its object. This is what Socrates now attacks by establishing an intimate connection between pleasure and judgment. He does so in a lengthy argument, starting with the question how the soul comes by its true and false judgments.

Soc.: Wouldn't you say that it often happens that someone who cannot get a clear view because he is looking from a distance wants to make up his mind about what he sees?

Pro.: I would say so.

Soc.: And might he then not again raise another question for himself?

Pro.: What question?

d Soc.: "What could that be that appears to stand near that rock under a tree?"—Do you find it plausible that someone might say these words to himself when he sets his eyes on such appearances?

Pro.: Certainly.

Soc.: And might he not afterwards, as an answer to his own question, say to himself, "It is a man," and in so speaking, would get it right?

Pro.: No doubt.

Soc.: But he might also be mistaken and say that what he sees is a statue, the work of some herdsmen?

Pro.: Very likely.

e Soc.: But if he were in company, he might actually say out loud to his companion what he had told himself, and so what we earlier called judgment would turn into an assertion?

Pro.: To be sure.

Soc.: Whereas if he is alone, he entertains this thought by himself, and sometimes he may even resume his way for quite a long time with the thought in his mind?

Pro.: No doubt.

Soc.: But look, do you share my view on this?

Pro.: What view?

Soc.: That our soul in such a situation is comparable to a book?

Pro.: How so?

39 Soc.: If memory and perceptions concur with other impressions at a particular occasion, then they seem to me to inscribe words in our soul, as it were. And if what is written is true, then we form a true judgment and a true account of the matter. But if what our scribe writes is false, then the result will be the opposite of the truth.[1]

---

1. The truth and falsity are initially those of simple sense-perceptions. But the scribe in our soul does more than that; he inscribes long-term views about the world. These are true or false in the same sense as the simple statements, however: They depict the way the world is, or they fail to do so. Plato's present explanation of falsity as blurred vision (in particular or in general) does not answer all the questions raised in *Tht.* or *Sph.*; it only indicates how mistaken experiences come about.

PRO.: I quite agree, and I accept this way of putting it. *b*

SOC.: Do you also accept that there is another craftsman at work in our soul at the same time?

PRO.: What kind of craftsman?

SOC.: A painter who follows the scribe and provides illustrations to his words in the soul.

PRO.: How and when do we say he does this work?

SOC.: When a person takes his judgments and assertions directly from sight or any other sense-perception and then views the images he has formed inside himself, corresponding to those judgments and assertions. Or is it not something of this sort that is going on in us?[1] *c*

PRO.: Quite definitely.

SOC.: And are not the pictures of the true judgments and assertions true, and the pictures of the false ones false?

PRO.: Certainly.

SOC.: If we have been right with what we have said so far, let us in addition come to terms about this question.

PRO.: What about?

SOC.: Whether these experiences are necessarily confined to the past and the present, but are not extended into the future.

PRO.: They should apply equally to all the tenses: past, present, and future.

SOC.: Now, did we not say before, about the pleasures and pains that *d* belong to the soul alone, that they might precede those that go through the body? It would therefore be possible that we have anticipatory pleasures and pains about the future.

PRO.: Undeniably.

SOC.: And are those writings and pictures which come to be in us, as we said earlier, concerned only with the past and the present, but not with *e* the future?

PRO.: Decidedly with the future.

SOC.: If you say 'decidedly', is it because all of them are really hopes for future times, and we are forever brimful of hopes, throughout our lifetime?

PRO.: Quite definitely.

---

1. The 'painter' in our soul represents not just an additional psychological observation. The existence of accurate or inaccurate images in our soul ensures that we can project such pleasures into the future, anticipating true and false pleasures. Without such pictures of imagination, my anticipated pleasure of eating cake would not be the real-life pleasure of *eating cake*. Problems with this view and objections to Plato's conception of true and false pleasures are discussed in Introd. p. xlv–viii.

Soc.: Well, then, in addition to what has been said now, also answer this question.

Pro.: Concerning what?

Soc.: Is not a man who is just, pious, and good in all respects, also loved by the gods?

Pro.: How could he fail to be?

Soc.: But what about someone who is unjust and in all respects evil? Isn't
40 he that man's opposite?

Pro.: Of course.

Soc.: And is not everyone, as we just said, always full of many hopes?

Pro.: Certainly.

Soc.: There are, then, assertions in each of us that we call hopes?

Pro.: Yes.

Soc.: But there are also those painted images. And someone often envisages himself in the possession of an enormous amount of gold and of a lot of pleasures as a consequence. And in addition, he also sees, in this inner picture himself, that he is beside himself with delight.[1]

b Pro.: What else!

Soc.: Now, do we want to say that in the case of good people these pictures are usually true, because they are dear to the gods, while quite the opposite usually holds in the case of wicked ones, or is this not what we ought to say?[2]

Pro.: That is just what we ought to say.

Soc.: And wicked people nevertheless have pleasures painted in their minds, even though they are somehow false?

Pro.: Right.

c Soc.: So wicked people as a rule enjoy false pleasures, but the good among mankind true ones?

Pro.: Quite necessarily so.

Soc.: From what has now been said, it follows that there are false pleasures in human souls that are quite ridiculous imitations of true ones, and also such pains.[3]

---

1. Socrates had mentioned earlier the difference in different people's pleasures (12d). This is now fully explained.

2. It is not likely that Plato is merely referring to the common (but also much disputed) Greek folk wisdom that those whom the gods love are those who prosper in life. He must also be implying that the *moral content* of foolish pleasures is mistaken, so that they represent a skewed view of life (cf. *Sph.* 228a–e on vice and deformity of the soul).

3. The fact that they are "ridiculous imitations" proves that Plato is not talking here of fundamentally different kinds, such as the philosopher's pleasures vs. the ordinary person's

PRO.: There certainly are.

SOC.: Now, it was agreed that whoever judges anything at all is always *really* judging, even if it is not about anything existing in the present, past, or future.

PRO.: Right.

SOC.: And these were, I think, the conditions that produce a false judgment *d* and judging falsely, weren't they?

PRO.: Yes.

SOC.: But should we not also grant to pleasures and pains a condition that is analogous in these ways?

PRO.: In what ways?

SOC.: In the sense that whoever has any pleasure at all, however ill-founded it may be, really does have pleasure, even if sometimes it is not about anything that either is the case or ever was the case, or often (or perhaps most of the time) refers to anything that ever will be the case.[1]

PRO.: That also must necessarily be so. *e*

SOC.: And the same account holds in the case of fear, anger, and everything of that sort, namely that all of them can at times be false?

PRO.: Certainly.

SOC.: Well, then, do we have any other way of distinguishing between bad and good judgments than their falsity?

PRO.: We have no other.

SOC.: Nor, I presume, will we find any other way to account for badness in the case of pleasures unless they are false.

PRO.: What you say is quite the opposite of the truth, Socrates! It is not *41* at all because they are false that we regard pleasures or pains as bad, but because there is some other grave and wide-ranging kind of badness involved.[2]

---

pleasures. As is soon pointed out, ridiculous pleasures are false enjoyment of nonexistent beauty, wealth, or cleverness (48d–49a).

1. Socrates concentrates on false pleasures about the future because these pleasures of anticipation are free from an involvement with the body. That makes it easier to show that the propositional content is false, not the things themselves that are enjoyed. That the omnitemporality of this falseness is emphasized shows that present and past pleasures also have propositional content and can be false in the same sense.

2. Once he has admitted the possibility of censoring pleasures, Protarchus sees that there are worse flaws in pleasure and pain than factual error. His next answer shows, however, that he is not yet quite comfortable with false pleasures. Badness rather than error comes up when the mixed pleasures are discussed (44d ff.).

SOC.: But let us discuss bad pleasures and what badness there is in their case a little later, if we still feel like it. Now we have to take up false pleasures in another sense and show that there is a great variety that arise and are at work in us. This argument will perhaps come in handy later,
b when we have to make our decisions.

PRO.: That may well be so, at least if there are any such pleasures.

SOC.: There certainly are, Protarchus; I at least am convinced. But until this is our accepted opinion, we cannot leave this conviction unexamined.

PRO.: Right.

SOC.: So let us get ready like athletes to form a line of attack around this problem.

PRO.: Here we go.

SOC.: We did say a short while ago in our discussion, as we may recall,
c that when what we call desires are in us, then body and soul part company and have each their separate experiences.

PRO.: We do remember, that was said before.

SOC.: And wasn't it the soul that had desires, desires for conditions opposite to the actual ones of the body, while it was the body that undergoes the pain or the pleasure of some affection?[1]

PRO.: That was indeed so.

SOC.: Draw your conclusions as to what is going on here.

PRO.: You tell me.

d SOC.: What happens is this: Under these circumstances pains and pleasures exist side by side, and there are simultaneously opposite perceptions of them, as we have just made clear.[2]

PRO.: Yes, that is clear.

SOC.: But did we not also discuss this point and come to an agreement how to settle it earlier?

PRO.: What point?

SOC.: That the two of them, both pleasure and pain, admit the more and less and belong to the unlimited kind?

PRO.: That was what we said. What about it?

---

1. That pleasure and pain are also experienced by *the body* is only a loose way of referring to the immediate feelings of deprivation and replenishment. There is no difficulty (*pace* Hackforth, l.c. 78) about pleasures of the body, independent of desire: While I enjoy eating, my soul may yet desire more and more.

2. There is at the same time the comprehension of the present pain as well as of its future assuagement (or vice versa: I may enjoy my present dinner and simultaneously fear its aftereffects).

SOC.: Do we have any means of making a right decision about these matters?

PRO.: Where and in what respect?   *e*

SOC.: In the case where we intend to come to a decision about any of them in such circumstances, which one is greater or smaller, or which one is more intensive or stronger: pain compared to pleasure, or pain compared to pain, or pleasure to pleasure.

PRO.: Yes, these questions do arise, and that is what we want to decide.

SOC.: Well, then, does it happen only to eyesight that seeing objects from afar or close by distorts the truth and causes false judgments? Or does not   *42* the same thing happen also in the case of pleasure and pain?[1]

PRO.: Much more so, Socrates.

SOC.: But this is the reverse of the result we reached a little earlier.

PRO.: What are you referring to?

SOC.: Earlier it was true and false *judgments* which affected the respective pleasures and pains with their own condition.

PRO.: Quite right.   *b*

SOC.: But now it applies to pleasures and pains themselves;[2] it is because they are alternately looked at from close up or far away, or simultaneously put side by side, that the pleasures seem greater compared to pain and more intensive, and pains seem, on the contrary, moderate in comparison with pleasures.

PRO.: It is quite inevitable that such conditions arise under these circumstances.

SOC.: But if you take that portion of them by which they appear greater or smaller than they really are, and cut it off from each of them as a   *c* X mere appearance and without real being, you will neither admit that this appearance is right nor dare to say that anything connected with this portion of pleasure or pain is right and true.[3]

---

1. A good example is Esau's distorted anticipated pleasure in eating his pottage. His enormous present hunger (pain) inflates the pleasure of eating. The distant pain of his lost birthright seems small in comparison.

2. With propositional false pleasures there is error of judgment that makes them false. With the inflated pleasures the immediate feeling distorts our perspective and leads to false judgment about the pleasure's size and worth. The distorted vision is not yet a matter of the intellect's judgment, although it "infects it" (as Plato expresses it at 42a1). Plato here takes up the claim made in the *Prot.* (355e–357e) that an art of measurement is needed in order to judge the true size of pleasure and pain. The *Phlb.* does not share the view that virtue consists in such an art, although it may presuppose a proper estimate of this kind.

3. In the case of inflated pleasures and pains we may enjoy their true part, provided we scale down our estimate of their size or worth. Plato speaks as if we were enjoying a "false part"

Pro.: Certainly not.

Soc.: Next in order after these, we will find pleasures and pains in animals that are even falser than these, both in appearance and reality, if we approach them in this way.[1]

Pro.: What are they, and what is the way?

Soc.: It has by now been said repeatedly that it is a destruction of the nature of those entities through combinations and separations, through

d processes of filling and emptying, as well as certain kinds of growth and decay, that gives rise to pain and suffering, distress, and whatever else comes to pass that goes under such a name.

Pro.: Yes, that has often been said.

Soc.: But when things are restored to their own nature again, this restoration, as we established in our agreement among ourselves, is pleasure.

Pro.: Correct.

Soc.: But what if nothing of that sort happens to our body, what then?

Pro.: When could that ever happen, Socrates?[2]

e Soc.: Your objection is not to the point, Protarchus.

Pro.: How so?

Soc.: Because you do not prevent me from putting my question to you again.

Pro.: What question?

Soc.: If in fact nothing of that sort took place, I will ask you, what would necessarily be the consequence of this for us?

Pro.: You mean if the body is not moved in either direction, Socrates?

Soc.: That is my question.

Pro.: This much is clear, Socrates, that in such a case there would not be either any pleasure or pain at all.

43 Soc.: Very well put. But I guess what you meant to say is that we necessarily are always experiencing one or the other, as the wise men say. For everything is in an eternal flux, upward and downward.[3]

---

of pleasure (as we can spend more money than we have), but this is certainly only a figurative way of saying that we enjoy a pleasure *as* greater than is actually warranted.

1. These false pleasures are not pleasures at all. Socrates is here unravelling the confusions of an ascetic who defines the undisturbed "third state" as pleasure.

2. The philosophically untrained Protarchus now learns the importance of "what if" questions. In addition it is indicated that an undisturbed life is not as opposed to reality as it might appear. A godlike state is at least conceivable (cf. 33b, 21e).

3. Socrates is alluding to the Heraclitean Flux theory, as it is commonly conceived. In contrast to many other such occasions, it does not represent a serious obstacle, because for

Pro.: They do say that, and what they say seems important.

Soc.: How else, since they themselves are important people? But I do want to avoid this argument which now assails us. I plan to escape it in this way, and you'd better make your escape with me.

Pro.: Just tell me how.

Soc.: "So be it," we will reply to them. But as for you, answer me this question: whether all living creatures in all cases notice it whenever they are affected in some way, so that we notice when we grow or experience anything of that sort, or whether it is quite otherwise. *b*

Pro.: It is indeed quite otherwise. Almost all of these processes totally escape our notice.

Soc.: But then what we just agreed to was not well spoken, that the changes 'upwards and downwards' evoke pleasures and pains.

Pro.: How could it?

Soc.: But if it is stated in this way, it will be better and become unobjec- *c* tionable.

Pro.: In what way?

Soc.: That great changes cause pleasures and pains in us, while moderate or small ones engender neither of the two effects.[1]

Pro.: That is more correct than the other statement, Socrates.

Soc.: But if this is correct, then we are back with the same kind of life we discussed before.

Pro.: What kind?

Soc.: The life that we said was painless, but also devoid of charm.

Pro.: Undeniably.

Soc.: So we end up with three kinds of life, the life of pleasure, the life *d* of pain, and the neutral life. Or what would you say about these matters?

Pro.: I would put it in the same way, that there are three kinds of life.

Soc.: But to be free of pain would not be the same thing as to have pleasure?

Pro.: How could it be the same?

Soc.: If you hear someone say that it is the most pleasant thing of all to live one's whole life without pain, how do you understand the speaker's intention?

---

once everyday experience suffices to disarm it: The fact that the continuous changes in the body escape our notice shows that, at least in principle, a neutral state is possible.

1. The discussion of the Flux theory was not superfluous. It leads to an important modification of the definition of pleasure and pain: Only drastic changes are their cause (cf. also the explanation at *Ti.* 64d–e of why sense-perception usually causes neither pleasure nor pain).

PRO.: To my understanding he seems to identify pleasure with freedom from pain.

e SOC.: Now, imagine three sorts of things, whichever you may like, and because these are high-sounding names, let us call them gold, silver, and what is neither of the two.

PRO.: Consider it done.

SOC.: Is there any way conceivable in which this third kind could turn out to be the same as one of our other two sorts, gold or silver?

PRO.: How could it?

SOC.: That the middle kind of life could turn out to be either pleasant or painful would be the wrong thing to think, if anyone happened to think so, and it would be the wrong thing to say, if anyone should say so, according to the proper account of the matter?

PRO.: No doubt.

44 SOC.: But we do find people who both think so and say so, my friend.

PRO.: Certainly.

SOC.: And do they really believe they experience pleasure when they are not in pain?

PRO.: They say so, at any rate.

SOC.: They believe therefore that they are pleased at that time. Otherwise they would not say that they are.[1]

PRO.: It looks that way.

SOC.: But they hold a false judgment about pleasure, if in fact freedom from pain and pleasure each have a nature of their own.

PRO.: But they do have their own.

SOC.: What decision shall we make? That there are three states in us, as

b we said just now, or that there are only two: pain being an evil in human life, and liberation from pain, also called pleasure, being the good as such?

PRO.: But why is it that we are asking ourselves this question now, Socrates? I don't get the point.

SOC.: That is because you don't really understand who the enemies of our Philebus here are.

PRO.: What enemies do you mean?

---

1. The claim of the impossibility of falsely believing we have pleasure or pain (36e) is therefore wrong, although the mistake is one in *theory*: Socrates' pseudohedonist (or antihedonist, as he turns out to be) is mistaken about what pleasure is, not about his own experiences. The clear separation of pleasure, pain, and the neutral state represents a correction of Plato's own somewhat confused views in *R.* IX, where he doubts that the process of restoration should be called pleasure, but calls it illusory and bastard pleasure (568b; 587b; on the unclarities of that position cf. D. Frede (1985), 158–161).

SOC.: I mean people with a tremendous reputation in natural science who say that there are no such things as pleasures at all.[1]

PRO.: How so?

SOC.: They hold that everything the followers of Philebus call pleasures are nothing but escape from pain.   *c*

PRO.: Do you suggest we should believe them, Socrates, or what is it you want us to do?

SOC.: Not that, but to use them as seers who make their prophecies, not in virtue of any art but in virtue of a certain harshness in their nature. It is a nature not without nobility, but out of an inordinate hatred that they have conceived against the power of pleasure, they refuse to acknowledge anything healthy in it, even to the point that they regard its very attractiveness itself as witchcraft rather than pleasure. You may now make use of them for our purposes, taking notice of the rest of their complaints that   *d* result from their harshness. After that you will hear what I, for my part, regard as true pleasures, so that through an examination of these two opposed points of view, we can reach a decision about the power of pleasure.

PRO.: A fair proposal.

SOC.: Let us attach ourselves to them as to allies and follow their traces in the direction in which their dour arguments point us.[2] I think they employ reasoning of this kind, starting from some such basic principle: If we wanted to know the nature of any character, like that of hardness,   *e* would we get a better understanding if we looked at the hardest kinds of things rather than at what has a low degree of hardness? Now, it is your task, Protarchus, to answer these difficult people, just as you answered me.

---

1. Different suggestions as to who the difficult person might be are discussed in Introd. p. l. Hackforth may be right that "we must be content to leave the *dyschereis* unidentified." That there was, nevertheless, such a person is very likely, for in *R.* IX 584a–b Plato refers to the unreality of the pleasure of restoration and applies the word "witchcraft" (*goeteia*), just as he does in *Phlb.* 44c9.

2. The antihedonist turns out to have made a fruitful mistake. By following up the real reason for his complaint, the partners discover yet another falseness connected with pleasure. Quite reasonably, he had taken the most intensive pleasures to be typical of all of them. However, the most intense pleasures have an important flaw: They are not only mixed with pain but *intensified* by pain. The complaint that pleasures mixed with pain are not real (= sheer) pleasures also applies to most pleasures of restoration, such as hunger and thirst. These are not the ones on which Socrates focuses here, but he includes them later, 47c–d.

PRO.: Gladly, and my answer to them will be that I would look at hardness of the first degree.

SOC.: But again if we wanted to study the form of pleasure, to see what
45 kind of nature it has, in that case we ought not to look at low-level pleasures, but at those that are said to be the strongest and most intensive.

PRO.: Everyone would grant you this point.

SOC.: Now, aren't the most immediate and greatest among the pleasures the ones connected with the body, as we have often said?

PRO.: No doubt.

SOC.: And is it the case that pleasures are more intensive or set in with greater intensity when people suffer from an illness than when they are healthy? We have to beware of a hasty answer here, lest we
b get tripped up. Perhaps we might be inclined to affirm this rather for the healthy people?

PRO.: Quite likely.

SOC.: But what about this? Are not those pleasures overwhelming which are also preceded by the greatest desires?

PRO.: That is certainly true.

SOC.: And when people suffer from fever or any such disease, aren't they more subject to thirst, chill, and whatever else continues to affect them through the body? Do they not feel greater deprivations, and also greater pleasures at their replenishment? Or shall we deny that this is true?

PRO.: It seems undeniable as you explained it now.

c SOC.: Very well. Are we justified, then, if we claim that whoever wants to study the greatest pleasures should turn to sickness, not to health? Now, mind you, my question was not whether the very sick have *more* pleasures than healthy people; my concern is rather with the size and *intensity* of the condition when it takes place. Our task, as we said, is to comprehend both what its true nature is and how those conceive of it who deny that there is any such thing as pleasure at all.[1]

d PRO.: I am following quite well what you say.

SOC.: You might as well be its guide, Protarchus. Now, tell me. Do you recognize greater pleasures in a life given to excesses—I do not say more pleasures, but pleasures that exceed by their force and intensity—than in a moderate life? Think carefully about it before you answer.

---

1. The morbid pleasures are the greatest because the desire for them is intensified by the magnitude of the deprivation or disturbance. This does not contradict Socrates' reservations whether sick people have *more* pleasures, because the morbid conditions and intensity of those pleasures does not make them more frequent; it may in fact make them less repeatable than healthy pleasures.

PRO.: I quite understand what you are after; I see indeed a huge difference. The moderate people somehow always stand under the guidance of the proverbial maxim "nothing too much" and obey it. But as to foolish people *e* and those given to debauchery, the excesses of their pleasures drive them near madness and to shrieks of frenzy.

SOC.: Good. But if this is how it stands, then it is obvious that it is in some vicious state of soul and body and not in virtue that the greatest pleasures as well as the greatest pains have their origin.

PRO.: Obviously.

SOC.: So we must pick out some of them to find out what characteristic of theirs made us call them the greatest.

PRO.: Necessarily. *46*

SOC.: Now, look at the pleasures that go with these types of maladies, what kinds of conditions they are.

PRO.: What types do you mean?

SOC.: Those pleasures of a rather repugnant type, which our harsh friends hate above all.

PRO.: What kinds?

SOC.: For example, the relief from itching by rubbing, and all of that sort that needs no other remedy.[1] But if this condition should befall us, what in heaven's name should we call it, pleasure or pain?

PRO.: That really would seem to be a mixed experience, with a bad component, Socrates.

SOC.: I did not raise this question with the intention of alluding to Philebus. *b* But without a clarification of these pleasures and of those who cultivate them, we could hardly come to any resolution of our problem.

PRO.: Then let us take up the whole tribe of these pleasures.

SOC.: You mean the ones that have that mixed nature?

PRO.: Right.

SOC.: There are mixtures that have their origin in the body and are confined to the body; then, there are mixtures found in the soul, and they *c* are confined to the soul. But then we will also find mixtures of pleasures and pains in both soul and body, and at one time the combination of both will be called pleasure; at other times it will be called pain.[2]

---

1. The itching and scratching of *Grg.* 494a–b reappears here, as well as the allusion to sexual activities, here combined with a reference to Philebus himself. Philebus is here (by innuendo) described as a mindless profligate (47b).

2. Those confined to the body must be those like itching and scratching or other purely physical states; the mixed pleasures of the soul will be discussed later (47d5 ff.). What are the mixed pleasures of soul and body? Plato discusses them at the end of this passage (47c–

PRO.: How so?

SOC.: When someone undergoes restoration or destruction he experiences two opposed conditions at once. He may feel hot while shivering or feel chilled while sweating. I suppose he will then want to retain one of these
d conditions and get rid of the other. But if this so called bittersweet condition is hard to shake, it first causes irritation and later on turns into wild excitement.

PRO.: A very accurate description.

SOC.: Now, isn't it the case that some of those mixtures contain an even amount of pleasures and pain, while there is a preponderance of either of the two in others?

PRO.: Right.

SOC.: Take the case that we just mentioned, of itching and scratching, as an example where the pains outweigh the pleasures. Now, when the
e irritation and infection are inside and cannot be reached by rubbing and scratching, there is only a relief on the surface.* In case they treat these parts by exposing them to fire or its opposite—they go from one extreme to the other in their distress—they sometimes procure enormous pleasures. But sometimes this leads to a state inside that is opposite to that outside, with a mixture of pains and pleasures, whichever way the balance may turn, because this treatment disperses by force what was mixed
47 together or mixes together what was separate, so that pains arise besides the pleasures.[1]

PRO.: Necessarily.

SOC.: Now, in all those cases where the mixture contains a surplus of pleasure, the small admixture of pain gives rise only to a tickle and a mild irritation, while the predominant part of pleasure causes contractions of the body to the point of leaping and kicking, color changes of all sorts, distortion of features, and wild palpitations; it finally drives the person totally out of his mind, so that he shouts aloud like a madman.

b PRO.: Very much so.

---

d); he makes clear that he is indeed including all pleasures and pains where expectation of the opposite state is involved, as in hunger. Are these also morbid states? They are, if the expectation of fulfillment increases the pain, and the pain the expectation.

1. Plato's theory that prolonged irritations (and pleasures) are caused when the remedies do not really reach the source is an interesting one; it seems to incorporate medical theories of his time, as may the explanation that, in the case of such morbid pleasures, the overall balance decides whether we call them pleasures rather than pains.

* Following Diès in leaving out Burnet's insertion of *en tois*.

SOC.: And this state causes him and others to say of him that he is almost dying of these pleasures. And the more profligate and mindless he is, the more will he pursue them by any means possible, and he calls them supreme and considers as the happiest of all mortals whoever lives in continuous enjoyment of them, as much as that is possible.

PRO.: Your description fits exactly the preconceptions of the common run of people, Socrates.

SOC.: Yes, as far as concerns the pleasures that arise when there is a *c* mixture of the external and internal state of the body, Protarchus. But take now the cases where the soul's contributions are opposed to the body's: When there is pain over and against pleasures, or pleasure against pain, both are finally joined in a mixed state. We have talked about them earlier and agreed that in these cases it is the deprivation that gives rise to the desire for replenishment, and while the expectation is pleasant, the deprivation itself is painful. When we discussed this we did not make any special mention, as we do now, of the fact that, in the vast number of cases *d* where soul and body are not in agreement, the final result is a single mixture that combines pleasure and pain.

PRO.: I suspect that you are right.

SOC.: But here we are still left with one further kind of mixture of pleasure and pain.

PRO.: Tell me what it is.

SOC.: The case, a common one, where the mixture is the product of affections within the soul itself, as we said before.[1]

PRO.: What was it again that we said?

SOC.: Take wrath, fear, longing, lamentations, love, jealousy, malice, and *e* other things like that; don't you regard them as a kind of pain within the soul itself?

PRO.: I certainly do.

SOC.: And don't we find that they are full of marvellous pleasures? Or do we need the famous lines as a reminder about wrath:

> ... That can embitter even the wise
> ... But much sweeter than soft-flowing honey ...[2]

---

1. The discussion suggests that for Plato all emotions are cases of pleasure mixed with pain. Unfortunately he does not explain what his reasons are, especially in the case of the negative emotions. He must presuppose that in all these states there is always the *expectation* of alleviation mixed in (in wrath for revenge, in longing for fulfillment).

2. Homer, *Il.* 18.108–9.

48 Similarly, in the case of lamentations and longing, aren't there also pleasures mixed in with the pain?
PRO.: No need for further reminders; in all these cases it must be just as
you said.
SOC.: And the same happens in those who watch tragedies: There is
laughter mixed with the weeping, if you remember.
PRO.: How could I forget?
SOC.: Now, look at our state of mind in comedy. Don't you realize that it
also involves a mixture of pleasure and pain?[1]
PRO.: I don't quite see that yet.
b SOC.: It is indeed not quite so easy to see that this condition applies under
those circumstances.
PRO.: It certainly is not to me!
SOC.: Since it is such an obscure matter, let us be all the more careful.
For this will help us to recognize more easily when there is a mixture of
pain and pleasure in other cases as well.
PRO.: Please tell me.
SOC.: Since we just mentioned the word "malice": Do you treat malice as
a pain of the soul, or what?[2]
PRO.: I do.
SOC.: On the other hand, will not the malicious person display pleasure
at his neighbor's misfortunes?
c PRO.: Very much so.
SOC.: Now, ignorance is a vice, and so is what we call stupidity?
PRO.: Decidedly!
SOC.: What conclusions do you draw from this about the nature of the
ridiculous?
PRO.: You tell me.
SOC.: It is, in sum, a kind of vice that derives its name from a special
disposition; it is, among all the vices, the one with a character* that stands

1. As Protarchus' reaction shows, comic delight is typically regarded as sheer pleasure. So
Plato picks a hard case to prove his point. He shows that such delight presupposes some
kind of resentment against others, for otherwise we would not enjoy their folly. For a further
discussion of *Schadenfreude,* cf. Introd. lii–liii.
2. "Malice" rather than "envy" seems the right translation for *phthonos,* because there is no
particular good we grudge others when we nevertheless feel satisfaction at their making fools
of themselves. It seems that for Plato all positive emotions have their negative background
(lack, need); otherwise we would be in a state of divine imperturbedness.

* Inserting *to* before *tounantion* in 48c8 with Diès.

in direct opposition to the one recommended by the famous inscription in Delphi.

PRO.: You mean the one that says "Know thyself," Socrates?

SOC.: I do. The opposite recommendation would obviously be that we not   *d*
know ourselves at all.*

PRO.: No doubt.

SOC.: Go on and make a subdivision of this disposition into three, Protarchus.

PRO.: What do you mean? I am afraid I don't know how to.

SOC.: Are you saying that it is up to me to make this division now?

PRO.: That is indeed what I am saying, but in addition I beg you to do so.

SOC.: Are there not necessarily three ways in which it is possible not to know oneself?

PRO.: What are they?

SOC.: The first way concerns money, if someone thinks himself richer   *e*
than he in fact is.

PRO.: Many people certainly share that condition.

SOC.: Even more consider themselves taller and handsomer than they in fact are, and believe they have other such physical advantages.

PRO.: Definitely.

SOC.: But an overwhelming number are mistaken about the third kind, which belongs to the soul, namely virtue, and believe that they are superior in virtue, although they are not.

PRO.: Very much so.

SOC.: And, again, among the virtues, is it not especially to wisdom that   49
the largest number of people lay claim, puffing themselves up with quarrels and false pretensions to would-be knowledge?[1]

PRO.: Undeniably so.

SOC.: It would therefore be quite justified to say that all these conditions are bad.

PRO.: Quite justified.

SOC.: So we must continue with our division of ignorance, Protarchus, if we want to find out what a strange mixture of pleasure and pain this comic malice is. How would you suggest that we should further subdivide? In   *b*
the case of all those who have such a false opinion about themselves, is it

---

1. Would-be beauty, wealth, or wisdom are the laughingstock in comedy.

---

* It is better to delete *legomenon hupo tou grammatos*, with Beck and Diès, as an awkward and pointless repetition of 48c8–9.

not most necessary, as it is for all mankind, that it be combined either with strength and power, or with its opposite?

PRO.: Necessarily.

SOC.: So make this the point of division. All those who combine this delusion with weakness and are unable to avenge themselves when they are laughed at, you are justified in calling ridiculous. But as for those who do have the power and strength to take revenge, if you call them dangerous

c and hateful, you are getting exactly the right conception about them. For ignorance on the side of the strong and powerful is odious and ugly; it is harmful even for their neighbors, both the ignorance itself and its imitations, whatever they may be.[1] Ignorance on the side of the weak, by contrast, deserves to be placed among the ridiculous in rank and nature.

PRO.: You are right about this division. But I am still not quite clear about where there is a mixture of pleasure and pain in these cases.

SOC.: So take first the nature of malice.

PRO.: Please explain.

d SOC.: It contains a kind of unjust pain and pleasure.[2]

PRO.: Necessarily.

SOC.: Now, if you rejoice about evils that happen to your enemy, is there any injustice or malice in your pleasure?

PRO.: How should there be?

SOC.: But is there any occasion when it is not unjust to be pleased rather than pained to see bad things happen to your friends?

PRO.: Clearly not.

SOC.: But we just agreed that ignorance is bad for everyone?

PRO.: Right.

SOC.: Let us take now the ignorance of friends which we said came in

e three versions, would-be wisdom and would-be beauty, and the other sort we just mentioned, each of which is ridiculous if weak, but odious if strong. Now, are we ready to affirm of our friends' state what we just said, namely, that it is ridiculous if it is harmless to others?

PRO.: Very much so.

SOC.: But did we not agree that it is bad if it is ignorance?

PRO.: We certainly did.

SOC.: But if we laugh about it, are we pleased or pained by it?

---

1. We refrain from *Schadenfreude* in the case of the strong, because their vices will have bad effects on ourselves. So such strong people are found not in comedy but in tragedy.

2. Our friends and neighbors don't deserve malice from us; therefore it is unjust to laugh at them.

PRO.: We are pleased, obviously.   *50*
SOC.: But this pleasure in the face of the misfortunes of friends—did we
not say that it was the product of malice?
PRO.: Necessarily.
SOC.: Our argument leads to the conclusion that if we laugh at what is ridiculous
about our friends, by mixing pleasure with malice, we thereby mix pleasure with   ᵡ
pain.[1] For we had agreed earlier that malice is a pain in the soul, that laughing
is a pleasure, and that both occur together on those occasions.
PRO.: True.
SOC.: The upshot of our discussion, then, is that in lamentations as well   *b*
as in tragedies and comedies, not only on stage but also in all of life's
tragedies and comedies, pleasures are mixed with pains, and so it is on
infinitely other occasions.
PRO.: It would be impossible not to agree with this, even for the most
ambitious defense of the opposite position, Socrates.
SOC.: Now, we had on our list of examples wrath, longing, lamentations,
fear, love, jealousy, malice, and whatever else, and we said that in these   *c*
cases we would discern the mixture that we have already mentioned so
frequently, right?
PRO.: Right.
SOC.: So we understand, then, that our whole explanation also applies to
longing, malice, and wrath?
PRO.: How could we fail to understand that?
SOC.: And there are many other such cases to which it applies?
PRO.: A great many.
SOC.: Now, what precisely do you think was the purpose for which I
pointed out to you this mixture in comedy? Don't you see that it was
designed to make it easier to persuade you that there is such a mixture in   *d*
fear and love and other cases?[2] I hoped that once you had accepted this
you would release me from a protracted discussion of the rest—once the
main point was understood, that there exists the possibility, for the body
without the soul, for the soul without the body, and for both of them in
a joint affection, to contain a mixture of pleasure and pain.
   Now, tell me whether you will let me go now or whether you will keep
us up till midnight. One further remark will gain me my release, I hope.
I will gladly give you a full account of the rest tomorrow, but for now I   *e*

1. Plato calls all negative attitudes pains. Ill will is a kind of negative emotional state.
2. This summary diagnosis concerning the emotions prepares the way for the selection of
the pure pleasures and makes clear why an emotional life is a mixed blessing.

want to steer towards the remaining points needed to make the decision
Philebus demands of us.

PRO.: Well spoken, Socrates. Discuss the rest any way you like.

3. True pleasures (50e–55c)

SOC.: It seems natural, somehow, that we must proceed from the mixed
pleasures to the discussion of the *unmixed* ones.[1]

51 PRO.: A very good point.

SOC.: I will now try to explain them in turn. Although I am not really in
agreement with those who hold that all pleasures are merely release from
pain, I nevertheless treat them as witnesses, as I said before, to prove that
there are certain kinds that only seem to be pleasures, but are not so in
reality, and furthermore, that there are others that have the appearance of
enormous size and great variety, but which are in truth commingled with
pain or with respite from severe pains suffered by soul and body.

b PRO.: But, Socrates, what are the kinds of pleasures that one could rightly
regard as true?

SOC.: Those that are related to so-called pure colors and to shapes and
to most smells and sounds and in general all those that are based on
imperceptible and painless lacks, while their fulfillments are perceptible
and pleasant.[2]

PRO.: But really, Socrates, what are you talking about?

SOC.: What I am saying may not be entirely clear straightaway, but I'll try
c to clarify it. By the beauty of a shape, I do not mean what the many might
presuppose, namely that of a living being or of a picture. What I mean,
what the argument demands, is rather something straight or round and
what is constructed out of these with a compass, rule, and square, such
as plane figures and solids. Those things I take it are not beautiful in a
relative sense, as others are, but are by their very nature forever beautiful
by themselves. They provide their own specific pleasures that are not at
d all comparable to those of rubbing! And colors are beautiful in an analo-

---

1. The "falsity" discussed last, that of mixture with pain, is Plato's preoccupation in the
section on true pleasures. It is, from his point of view, the most important kind, because it
is the most disturbing one. Factually false or overrated pleasures don't have much attraction,
while the intensive ones do.

2. The condition of a *painless lack* for true pleasures confirms that all pleasures, even the
best ones, are "fillings" of some sort. This impression not only agrees with the general
definition of pleasure as a restoration of health and harmony, but it is also confirmed at 54d
by the general assurance that all pleasures are a kind of *generation*.

gous way and import their own kinds of pleasures. Do we now understand it better, or how do you feel?[1]

Pro.: I am really trying to understand, Socrates, but will you also try to say this more clearly?

Soc.: What I am saying is that those among the smooth and bright sounds that produce one pure note are not beautiful in relation to anything else but in and by themselves and that they are accompanied by their own pleasures, which belong to them by nature.

Pro.: That much is true.

Soc.: Then there is also the less divine tribe of pleasures connected with *e* smells. But because there is no inevitable pain mixed with them, in whatever way or wherever we may come by them, for this reason I regard them as the counterpart to those others. So, if you get my point, we will then treat those as two species of the kinds of pleasures we are looking for.[2]

Pro.: I do get your point.

Soc.: Then let us also add to these the pleasures of learning, if indeed *learning* we are agreed that there is no such thing as hunger for learning connected *52* with them, nor any pains that have their source in a hunger for learning.[3]

Pro.: Here, too, I agree with you.

Soc.: Well, then, if after such filling with knowledge, people lose it again through forgetting, do you notice any kinds of pain?

Pro.: None that could be called inherent by nature, but in our reflections on this loss when we need it, we experience it as a painful loss. *b*

Soc.: But, my dear, we are here concerned only with the natural affections themselves, apart from reflection on them.

1. It seems rather odd that only simple patches of pure color, geometrical shapes, and individual pure sounds and smells should be admitted as objects of pure pleasure. But they best satisfy the criterion of *completeness*, because their attractiveness does not depend on variety that breeds longing for further variety. So there is intrinsic moderation in such pleasures (52c–d; cf. *Phdr.* 250d).

2. Two species, because the more divine pleasures of pure sights and sounds are contrasted with the less divine one of smell. The lesser divinity of smells must be due to their less definite nature (cf. *Ti.* 66d–67a).

3. Intellectual pleasures are here strictly limited to learning, because only learning is a process. Learning is pleasant because it is the *filling* of an unfelt lack. That this is the point is confirmed by the insistence that neither the acquisition nor the loss of knowledge is accompanied by pain. That knowledge itself does not provide pleasure is assured at 55a, where the life of pure thought is assigned to the 'third life'. Plato has given up the notion, defended in *R.* IX with so much fanfare, that the philosopher outdoes everyone in the amount of pleasure he gains. He obviously came to realize that this is incompatible with the generic definition of pleasure as a *process*.

PRO.: Then you are right in saying that the lapse of knowledge never causes us any pain.

SOC.: Then we may say that the pleasures of learning are unmixed with pain and belong, not to the masses, but only to a very few?[1]

PRO.: How could one fail to agree?

c SOC.: But now that we have properly separated the pure pleasures and those that can rightly be called impure, let's add to our account the attribution of immoderation to the violent pleasures, but moderation, in contrast, to the others. That is to say, we will assign those pleasures which display high intensity and violence, no matter whether frequently or rarely, to the class of the unlimited, the more and less, which affects both body

d and soul. The other kinds of pleasures we will assign to the class of things that possess measurement.

PRO.: Quite right, Socrates.

SOC.: But we have also to look into the following question about them.

PRO.: What question?

SOC.: The question of their relation to truth. What is closer to it: the pure, unadulterated, and sufficient* or the violent, multiform, and enormous?

PRO.: Just what are you after in asking this question, Socrates?

e SOC.: I want to omit nothing in the investigation of both pleasure and knowledge. I want to ask if one part of them is pure, another impure, so that both of them may come to trial in their pure form, and so make it easier for you and me and all those present to come to a verdict in this trial.

PRO.: Quite right.

SOC.: Then let us go on and see whether all items that belong in the pure kind display the following qualification. But let us first pick out one of them and study it.

53 PRO.: Which one shall we choose?

SOC.: Let us take whiteness first, if you have no objection.

PRO.: That is fine with me.

SOC.: Now, how can there be purity in the case of whiteness, and what sort of thing is it? Is it the greatest quantity or amount, or is it rather the

---

1. The rationale must be that only those learn with pleasure and not with pain, for whom such an acquisition leads to a naturally harmonious state.

---

* Accepting the transposition of *to hikanon* with Jackson and Diès rather than Burnet's reading *itamon* for *hikanon*.

complete lack of any admixture, that is, where there is not the slightest part of any other kind contained in this color?

PRO.: It will obviously be the perfectly unadulterated color.

SOC.: Right. But shall we not also agree that this is the truest and the most beautiful of all instances of white, rather than what is greatest in quantity or amount? *b*

PRO.: Certainly.

SOC.: So we are perfectly justified if we say that a small portion of pure white is to be regarded as whiter than a larger quantity of an impure whiteness, and at the same time more beautiful and possessed of more truth?[1]

PRO.: Perfectly justified.

SOC.: Well, now, we don't need to run through many more examples to justify our account of pleasure, but this example suffices to prove that in the case of pleasure, too, every small and insignificant pleasure that is *c* unadulterated by pain will turn out to be pleasanter, truer, and more beautiful than a greater quantity and amount of the impure kind.[2]

PRO.: Quite definitely so, and the example is sufficient.

SOC.: But what about the following point? Have we not been told that pleasure is always a process of *becoming*, and that there is no *being* at all of pleasure? There are some subtle thinkers who have tried to pass on this doctrine to us, and we ought to be grateful to them.[3]

PRO.: What does it mean?

1. This argument is intended to establish that purity is the right criterion, while quantity is not. Only then can maximization be excluded. It had been shown that the greatest pleasures are not the best because they contain pain. Now Plato has to show that even painless pleasures with pure objects gain nothing by increase. He does not really argue for this: Protarchus simply accepts the suggestion that there is no increase in the pleasure of pure white if we have more of it. Although pleasure in itself remains an unlimited thing, these objects don't permit increase.

2. This is a disappointingly austere program, even if it is in agreement with Plato's principles. Its austerity surpasses that of Plato's criticism of the arts in the *Republic*. We must not forget, however, that the question is not what is permitted in life but what is an unqualified good.

3. This distinction between *being* and *becoming* is the conclusion of Plato's critique; having discussed various flaws in different kinds of pleasures, he finishes this part by reverting to its *generic* trait, which rules out that it can ever be perfect. Who are the "subtle thinkers" to whom Socrates expresses gratitude? The addressee is no doubt Plato himself (for the epithet *kompsos* as a term of recommendation, cf. *Phd.* 105c; *R.* 525d; *Tht.* 156a); the firm entrenchment of pleasure with generation is an innovation of the *Phlb.*, and this is solemnly acknowledged here.

SOC.: I will indeed try to explain it to you, my friend Protarchus, by
d resuming my questioning.

PRO.: You have only to keep on asking.

SOC.: Suppose there are two kinds of things, one kind sufficient to itself,
the other in need of something else.

PRO.: How and what sort of things do you mean?

SOC.: The one kind by nature possesses supreme dignity; the other is
inferior to it.

PRO.: Express this more clearly, please.

SOC.: We must have met handsome and noble youths, together with their
courageous lovers.[1]

PRO.: Certainly.

SOC.: Now, try to think of another set of two items that corresponds to
e this pair in all the relevant features that we just mentioned.

PRO.: Do I have to repeat my request for the third time? Please express
more clearly what it is you want to say, Socrates!

SOC.: Nothing fanciful at all, Protarchus; this is just a playful manner of
speaking. What is really meant is that all things are either for the sake of
something else or they are that for whose sake the other kind comes to be
in each case.

PRO.: I finally managed to understand it, thanks to the many repetitions.

54 SOC.: Perhaps, my boy, we will understand better as the argument proceeds.

PRO.: No doubt.

SOC.: So let's take another pair.

PRO.: Of what kind?

SOC.: Take on the one hand the *generation* of all things, on the other their
being.

PRO.: I also accept this pair from you, being and generation.

SOC.: Excellent. Now, which of the two do you think exists for the other's
sake? Shall we say that generation takes place for the sake of being, or
does being exist for the sake of generation?

PRO.: Whether what is called being is what it is for the sake of generation,
is that what you want to know?

SOC.: Apparently.

---

1. The example, unexpected and unexplained, recalls the doctrine of *Sym.* and the *Phdr.*,
where the lover is 'incomplete', a hunter for beauty, while the beloved represents perfection.
"We must have met" seems also intended to put Philebus at a distance, because he is not
such a noble youth but the symbol of immoderate love.

PRO.: By heavens, what a question to ask me! You might as well ask: "Tell   *b*
me, Protarchus, whether shipbuilding goes on for the sake of ships or
whether ships are for the sake of shipbuilding," or some such thing.

SOC.: That is precisely what I am talking about, Protarchus.

PRO.: What keeps you from answering your questions yourself, Socrates?

SOC.: Nothing, provided you take your share in the argument.

PRO.: I am quite determined to.

SOC.: I hold that all ingredients, as well as all tools, and quite generally all   *c*
materials, are always provided for the sake of some process of generation.
I further hold that every process of generation in turn always takes place
for the sake of some particular being, and that all generation taken together
takes place for the sake of the existence of being as a whole.

PRO.: Nothing could be clearer.

SOC.: Now, pleasure, since it is a process of generation, necessarily comes
to be for the sake of some being.

PRO.: Of course.

SOC.: But that for the sake of which what comes to be for the sake of
something comes to be in each case, ought to be put into the class of the
things good in themselves, while that which comes to be for the sake of
something else belongs in another class, my friend.

PRO.: Undeniably.   *d*

SOC.: But if pleasure really is a kind of generation, will we be placing it
correctly, if we put it in a class different from that of the good?

PRO.: That too is undeniable.

SOC.: It is true, then, as I said at the beginning of this argument, that we
ought to be grateful to the person who indicated to us that there is always
only generation of pleasure and that it has no being whatsoever. And it is
obvious that he will just laugh at those who claim that pleasure is good.[1]

PRO.: Certainly.   *e*

SOC.: But this same person will also laugh at those who find their fulfillment in processes of generation.

PRO.: How so, and what sort of people are you alluding to?

SOC.: I am talking of those who cure their hunger and thirst or anything
else that is cured by processes of generation. They take delight in genera-

1. Since Plato indicates no exception, this seems to include even the pure pleasures, as
accords well with their status of fillings of an *unfelt* lack. If they are good, this accrues to
them only on account of their objects' purity and moderation, not *qua* pleasures. So they are
good only contingently, as Plato had indicated (32c–d). That humans are always subject to
generation is here only suggested (complete 'being' is always the end of all generation), but
it will come up again when the ingredients for the good human life are selected.

tion as a pleasure and proclaim that they would not want to live if they
were not subject to hunger and thirst and if they could not experience all
the other things one might want to mention in connection with such
conditions.

55   PRO.: That is very like them.

SOC.: But would we not all say that destruction is the opposite of generation?

PRO.: Necessarily.

SOC.: So whoever makes this choice would choose generation and destruction in preference to that third life which consists of neither pleasure nor
pain, but is a life of thought in the purest degree possible.[1]

PRO.: So a great absurdity seems to appear, Socrates, if we posit pleasure
as good.

SOC.: An absurdity indeed, especially if we go on to look at it this way.

PRO.: In what way?

b   SOC.: How is this not absurd: that there should be nothing good or noble
in bodies or anywhere else except in the soul, but in the soul pleasure
should be the only good thing, so that courage or moderation or reason
or any of the other goods belonging to the soul would be neither good nor
noble? In addition, we would have to call the person who experiences not
pleasure but pain *bad* while he is in pain, even if he were the best of all
men. By contrast, we would have to say of whoever is pleased that the

c   greater his pleasure whenever he is pleased, the more he excels in virtue![2]

PRO.: All that is as absurd as possible, Socrates.

4. The critique of knowledge: pure and impure forms (55c–59d)

SOC.: Now, let us not undertake to give pleasure every possible test, while
going very lightly with reason and knowledge. Let us rather strike them
valiantly all around, to see if there is some fault anywhere. So we'll learn

---

1. Plato's preference for the life of 'being', were it possible, rather than a life of constant
generation and destruction, is confirmed here, once again. Philebus is the target here, with
his demand for increase of pleasure, but the passage also harks back to the discussion with
Callicles, who had explicitly welcomed the life of flux (*Grg.* 493d ff.).

2. This passage seems to be a kind of appendix, an afterthought that does not fit too well
where it stands. This *reductio ad absurdum* of what would happen if pleasure were the only
good should have come much earlier in the dialogue, if at all. It looks as if Plato had inserted
it after rereading *Grg.* 497d—thinking of Callicles may have brought this argument back to
mind.

what is by nature purest in them. And seeing this, we can use the truest parts of these, as well as of pleasure, to make our joint decision.[1]

PRO.: Fair enough.

SOC.: Among the disciplines to do with knowledge, one part is productive, *d* the other concerned with education and nurture, right?[2]

PRO.: Just so.

SOC.: But let us first find out whether within the manual arts there is one side more closely related to knowledge itself, the other less closely; secondly, whether we should treat the one as quite pure, as far as it goes, the other as less pure.

PRO.: That is what we ought to do.

SOC.: So let us sort out the leading disciplines among them.

PRO.: Which disciplines, and how are we to do it?

SOC.: If someone were to take away all counting, measuring, and weighing *e* from the arts and crafts, the rest might be said to be worthless.

PRO.: Worthless, indeed!

SOC.: All we would have left would be conjecture and the training of our senses through experience and routine. We would have to rely on our ability to make the lucky guesses that many people call art, once it has acquired some proficiency through practice and hard work. *56*

PRO.: Undeniably so.

SOC.: This is clear, to start with, in the case of flute-playing.* The harmonies are found not by measurement but by the hit and miss of training, and quite generally music tries to find the measure by observing the vibrating strings. So there is a lot of imprecision mixed up in it and very little reliability.[3]

PRO.: Very true.

---

1. "Truth" in application to knowledge is understood in terms of purity and accuracy. Knowledge can neither be false nor contain an admixture of its opposite, ignorance, although Plato indicates some admixture of impurity (59c) .

2. After this first dichotomy, the separation of the productive and the liberal arts, there is no further division of all the arts and sciences. The criterion of selection, accuracy, cuts across all disciplines. In what follows Plato shows, in a very rough manner, how mathematical accuracy determines the rank of the arts on each side of the dichotomy.

3. This recalls the reproach against the unscientific musicians in *R.* 531a–c.

---

* I accept with Diès the transposition of *autes auletikes* first suggested by Bury. Since flute-playing has nothing to do with measuring strings its position in the ms is rather awkward (it might be a gloss of someone wondering about the applicability to other forms of music).

b SOC.: And will we not discover that medicine, agriculture, navigation, and strategy are in the same condition?

PRO.: Definitely.

SOC.: But as to building, I believe that it owes its superior level of craftsmanship over other disciplines to its frequent use of measures and instruments, which give it high accuracy.

PRO.: In what way?

SOC.: In shipbuilding and housebuilding, but also in many other wood-
c working crafts. For it employs straightedge and compass, as well as a mason's rule, a line, and an ingenious gadget called a carpenter's square.

PRO.: You are quite right, Socrates.

SOC.: Let us, then, divide the so-called arts into two parts, those like music, with less precision in their practice, and those like building, with more precision.

PRO.: Agreed.

SOC.: And let's take those among them as most accurate that we called primary just now.

PRO.: I suppose you mean arithmetic and the other disciplines you mentioned after it.

d SOC.: That's right. But don't you think we have to admit that they, too, fall into two kinds, Protarchus?

PRO.: What two kinds do you mean?

SOC.: Don't we have to agree, first, that the arithmetic of the many is one thing, and the philosophers' arithmetic is quite another?

PRO.: How could anyone distinguish these two kinds of arithmetic?

SOC.: The difference is by no means small, Protarchus. First there are those who compute sums of quite unequal units, such as two armies or
e two herds of cattle, regardless whether they are tiny or huge. But then there are the others who would not follow their example, unless it were guaranteed that none of those infinitely many units differed in the least from any of the others.[1]

PRO.: You explain very well the notable difference among those who make numbers their concern, so it stands to reason that there are those two different kinds of arithmetic.

SOC.: Well, then, what about the art of calculating and measuring as

---

1. Plato had protested in *R.* VII 524d ff. against imprecision in mathematics, but here he goes further and separates pure and applied mathematics. The separation remains sketchy, however. It is not clear, for instance, whether "mathematics for architects" would remain one of the liberal arts (*paideia*) or cross over to the productive arts.

builders and merchants use them and the geometry and calculations practiced by philosophers—shall we say there is one sort of each of them or two?   *57*

PRO.: Going by what was said before, I ought to vote for the option that they are two of each sort.

SOC.: Right. But do you realize why we have brought up this question here?

PRO.: Possibly, but I would appreciate it if you answered the question yourself.

SOC.: The aim of our discussion now seems to be, just as it was when we first set out, to find an analogue here to the point we made about pleasure.   *b* So now we ought to find out whether there is a difference in purity between different kinds of knowledge in the same way as there was between different kinds of pleasures.

PRO.: This obviously was the purpose of our present question.

SOC.: But what next? Have we not discovered before that different subject matters require different arts and that they have different degrees of certainty?

PRO.: Yes, we did.

SOC.: It is questionable, then, whether an art that goes under one name and is commonly treated as one should not rather be treated as two, depending on the difference in certainty and purity. And if this is so, we   *c* must also ask whether the art has more precision in the hands of the philosopher than its counterpart in the hands of the nonphilosopher.

PRO.: That is indeed the question here.

SOC.: So what answer shall we give to it, Protarchus?

PRO.: Socrates, we have come across an amazing difference between the sciences, as far as precision is concerned.

SOC.: Will that facilitate our answer?

PRO.: Obviously. And let it be said that these sciences are far superior to the other disciplines, but that those among them that are animated by the   *d* spirit of the true philosophers are infinitely superior yet in precision and truth in their use of measure and number.

SOC.: Let us settle for this doctrine, and trusting you, we will confidently answer those powerful makers of word traps.[1]

PRO.: What answer shall we give them?

SOC.: That there are two kinds of arithmetic and two kinds of geometry,

---

1. Socrates pretends in jest that hunters for ambiguities might attack them if they make no clear decision about the two kinds of mathematics.

and a great many other sciences following in their lead, which have the
same twofold nature while sharing one name.

e PRO.: Let us give our answer, with best wishes, to those powerful people,
as you call them, Socrates.

SOC.: Do we maintain that these kinds of sciences are the most precise?

PRO.: Certainly.

SOC.: But the power of dialectic would repudiate us if we put any other
science ahead of her.

PRO.: What science do we mean by that again?

58 SOC.: Clearly everybody would know what science I am referring to now![1]
For I take it that anyone with any share in reason at all would consider
the discipline concerned with being and with what is really and forever in
every way eternally self-same by far the truest of all kinds of knowledge.
But what is your position? How would you decide this question, Protarchus?

PRO.: On many occasions, Socrates, I have heard Gorgias insist that the
art of persuasion is superior to all others because it enslaves all the rest,

b with their own consent, not by force, and is therefore by far the best of all
the arts. Now I am reluctant to take up a position against either him or
you.

SOC.: I suspect that at first you wanted to say "take up arms," but then
suppressed it in embarrassment.[2]

PRO.: You may take this whatever way pleases you.

SOC.: But am I to blame for a misunderstanding on your part?

PRO.: In what respect?

SOC.: What I wanted to find out here, my dear friend Protarchus, was not

c what art or science excels all others by its grandeur, by its nobility, or by
its usefulness to us. Our concern here was rather to find which one aims
for clarity, precision, and the highest degree of truth, even if it is a minor

---

1. "Dialectic" was used in passing in connection with the divine method (17a). It is questionable whether Plato is using it here in the same sense or whether he is indicating some change
(cf. *ge nun*). Since the divine method was applicable to all disciplines, he might have in mind
here an even higher employment (strictly limited to philosophers), or he might be indicating
that the method when properly employed deals with unchangeable being (cf. Introd. p. lviii–
lix). A distinction might also be intended between applied and philosophical dialectic (cf. the
'Prometheus' at 16c).

2. Socrates jokingly picks up on Gorgias' claim of (nonviolent) persuasion for rhetoric, so
speaking of "arms" would be an embarrassment. Protarchus has not given up his allegiance
to Gorgias, even though he is no longer an adherent to hedonism.

discipline and our benefit is small. Look at it this way: You can avoid making an enemy of Gorgias so long as you let his art win as far as the actual profit for human life is concerned.[1]

But as to the discipline I am talking about now, what I said earlier about the white also applies in this case: Even in a small quantity it can be superior in purity and truth to what is large in quantity but impure and *d* untrue. We must look for this science without concern for its actual benefit or its prestige, but see whether it is by its nature a capacity in our soul to love the truth and to do everything for its sake. And if thorough reflection and sufficient discussion confirms this for our art, then we can say that it is most likely to possess purity of mind and reason. Otherwise we would have to look for a higher kind of knowledge than this.

PRO.: Well, thinking it over, I agree that it would be difficult to find any *e* other kind of art or any other science that is closer to the truth than this one.

SOC.: When you gave this answer now, did you realize that most of the arts and sciences and those who work at them are in the first place only concerned with opinions and make opinions the center of their search? For *59* even if they think they are studying nature, you must realize that all their lives they are merely dealing with this world order, how it came to be, how it is affected, and how it acts?[2] Is that our position or not?

PRO.: Quite so.

SOC.: So such a person assumes the task of dealing, not with things eternal, but with what comes to be, will come to be, or has come to be?

PRO.: Undeniably.

SOC.: So how could we assert anything definite about these matters with exact truth if it never did possess nor will possess nor now possesses any *b* kind of sameness?

---

1. It has been suggested that this conciliatory attitude towards Gorgias represents a change of heart about rhetoric. If Socrates is not deeply ironic here, he is indeed far away from the Socrates who condemned rhetoric as flattery and denied it the status of an art (*Grg.* 462b ff.). This leniency towards rhetoric prepares us for his pragmatic approach towards all the arts in the selection of the components of the good life.

2. The difference between knowledge and belief comes up here for the first and only time. True belief had been mentioned among the better goods in the beginning (11b), and it is included with the other 'lesser sciences' in the final list of goods (66c). The contrast does not play much of a role here, because practical concerns of human life are at stake, but Plato at least wants to indicate that it has not been abandoned when it comes to the proper conception of knowledge.

PRO.: Impossible.

SOC.: And how could we ever hope to achieve any kind of certainty about subject matters that do not in themselves possess any certainty?[1]

PRO.: I see no way.

SOC.: Then there can be no reason or knowledge that attains the highest truth about these subjects!

PRO.: At least it does not seem likely.

SOC.: We must therefore dismiss entirely you and me and also Gorgias and Philebus, but must make this declaration about our investigation.[2]

c PRO.: What declaration?

SOC.: Either we will find certainty, purity, truth, and what we may call integrity among the things that are forever in the same state, without anything mixed in it, or we will find it in what comes as close as possible to it. Everything else has to be called second-rate and inferior.

PRO.: Very true.

SOC.: Would not strict justice demand that we call the noblest things by the noblest names?

PRO.: That's only fair.

d SOC.: And aren't reason and knowledge names that deserve the highest honor?

PRO.: Yes.

SOC.: So, in their most accurate sense and appropriate use, they are applied to insights into true reality?

PRO.: Definitely.

SOC.: But these were the very names that I put forward at the beginning for our verdict.

PRO.: The very ones, Socrates.

IV. The "synthetic" part of the discussion: mixing together the good life (59d–64b)

SOC.: Good. But as to the *mixture* of intelligence and pleasure, if one *e* likened our situation to that of builders with ingredients or materials to use in construction, this would be a fitting comparison.

1. The *Ti.* aspires to go beyond the accounts of generation and destruction by describing the eternal world order itself, even though it admits that it gives no more than a likely account.

2. All thought of partisanship (cf. *philonikia*, 14b) must by now be given up when it comes to admitting the superiority of reason and intelligence among intellectual activities. As Hackforth has rightly pointed out (l.c. 124n1), Plato has not kept *nous* and *phronesis* strictly separate from the other *epistemai*, nor does he do so in the last part, but that does not detract from his intention to separate higher and lesser disciplines.

PRO.: Very fitting.

SOC.: So next we ought to try our hands at the mixture?

PRO.: Definitely.

SOC.: But had we not better repeat and remind ourselves of certain points?

PRO.: What are they?

SOC.: Those we kept reminding ourselves of before. The proverb fits well here that says that good things deserve repeating 'twice or even thrice'.[1] *60*

PRO.: Definitely.

SOC.: On, then, by the heavens! This is, I think, the general drift of what we said.

PRO.: What was it?

SOC.: Philebus says that pleasure is the right aim for all living beings and that all should try to strive for it, that it is at the same time the good for all things, so that good and pleasant are but two names that really belong to what is by nature one and the same. Socrates, by contrast, affirms that *b* these are not one and the same thing but two, just as they are two in name, that the good and the pleasant have a different nature, and that intelligence has a greater share in the good than pleasure. Isn't that the matter at issue now, just as it was before, Protarchus?

PRO.: Very much so.

SOC.: And are we also agreed on this point now, just as we were before?

PRO.: What point?

SOC.: That the difference between the nature of the good and everything else is this?

PRO.: What is it? *c*

SOC.: Any creature that was in permanent possession of it, entirely and in every way, would never be in need of anything else, but would live in perfect self-sufficiency. Is that right?

PRO.: It is right.

SOC.: But didn't we try to give them a separate trial in our discussion, assigning each of them a life of its own, so that pleasure would remain unmixed with intelligence, and, again, intelligence would not have the tiniest bit of pleasure?

PRO.: That's what we did.

SOC.: Did either of the two seem to us self-sufficient at that time for *d* anyone?

PRO.: How could it?

---

1. The restatement of the whole case and of the criteria agreed on (20d) for the decision emphasizes Socrates' role as impartial judge.

Soc.: If some mistake was made then, anyone now has the opportunity to take it up again and correct it. Let him put memory, intelligence, knowledge, and true opinion into one class, and ask himself whether anybody would choose to possess or acquire anything else without that class. Most
e particularly, whether he would want pleasure, as much and as intensive as it can be, without true opinion that he enjoys it, without recognizing what kind of experience it is he has, without memory of this affection for any length of time. And let him put reason to the same test, whether anyone would prefer to have it without any kind of pleasure, even a very short-lived one, rather than with some pleasures, provided that he does not want all pleasures without intelligence rather than with some fraction of it.

Pro.: Neither of them will do, Socrates, and there is no need to raise the same question so often.

61 Soc.: So neither of these two would be perfect, worthy of choice for all, and the supreme good?

Pro.: How could they?

Soc.: The good therefore must be taken up precisely or at least in outline, so that, as we said before, we know to whom we will give the second prize.

Pro.: You are right.

Soc.: Have we not discovered at least a road that leads towards the good?

Pro.: What road?

Soc.: It's as if, when you are looking for somebody, you first find out
b where he actually lives. That would be a major step towards finding him.[1]

Pro.: No doubt.

Soc.: Similarly here. There is this argument which has now indicated to us, just as it did at the beginning of our discussion, that we ought not to seek the good in the unmixed life but in the mixed one.

Pro.: Quite.

Soc.: But there is more hope that what we are looking for will show itself in a well-mixed life rather than in a poorly mixed one?

Pro.: Much more.

Soc.: So let us pray to the gods for assistance when we perform our
c mixture, Protarchus, whether it be Dionysus or Hephaestus or any other deity who is in charge of presiding over such mixtures.

Pro.: By all means.

---

1. Although the mixed life is agreed to be the best (life), it is not identical with the Good as such. Therefore they have to find out first what mixture is best and then find the principle of its goodness.

Soc.: We stand like cup-bearers before the fountains—the fountain of pleasure, comparable to honey, and the sobering fountain of intelligence, free of wine, like sober, healthy water—and we have to see how to make a perfect mixture of the two.

Pro.: Certainly.

Soc.: But let's look first into this: Will our mixture be as good as it can *d* be if we mix every kind of pleasure with every kind of intelligence?[1]

Pro.: Maybe.

Soc.: It is not without risk, however. But now I have an idea how we might procure a safer mixture.

Pro.: Tell us what it is.

Soc.: Didn't we find that one pleasure turned out to be truer than another, just as one art was more precise than the other?

Pro.: Definitely.

Soc.: But there was also a difference between different sciences, since one kind deals with a subject matter that comes to be and perishes, the *e* other is concerned with what is free of that, the eternal and self-same. Since we made truth our criterion, the latter kind appeared to be the truer one.

Pro.: That was certainly so.

Soc.: If we took from each sort the segments that possess most truth and mixed them together, would this mixture provide us with the most desirable life, or would we also need less-true ones?

Pro.: We should do it this way, it seems to me. *62*

Soc.: Suppose, then, there is a person who understands what justice itself is and can give the appropriate definitions and possesses the same kind of comprehension about all the rest of what there is.

Pro.: Let that be presupposed.

Soc.: Will he be sufficiently versed in science if he knows the definition of the circle and of the divine sphere itself but cannot recognize the human sphere and these our circles, using even in housebuilding those other *b* yardsticks and those circles?[2]

Pro.: We would find ourselves in a rather ridiculous position if we were confined entirely to those divine kinds of knowledge, Socrates!

1. The general agreement on the mixture of pleasure and knowledge does not define what kinds of each are to go into it.

2. In spite of the 'divinity' assigned to the objects and the science itself, Plato cannot here mean the transcendent Forms alone, as they are dealt with by the philosopher, but must be referring to pure mathematics, etc. We should remember that pure sights and sounds were also called divine and that the proper method for all disciplines was also of divine origin.

Soc.: What are you saying? Ought we at the same time to include the inexact and impure science of the false yardstick and circle, and add it to the mixture?

Pro.: Yes, necessarily so, if any one of us ever wants to find his own way home.

c Soc.: But how about music: Ought we also to mix in the kind of which we said a little earlier that it is full of lucky hits and imitation but lacks purity?

Pro.: It seems necessary to me, if in fact our life is supposed to be at least some sort of *life*.

Soc.: Do you want me, then, to yield like a doorkeeper to the pushing and shoving of a crowd and to throw open the doors and let the flood of all sorts of knowledge in, the inferior kind mingling with the pure?

d Pro.: I for my part can't see what damage it would do to accept all the other kinds of knowledge, as long as we have those of the highest kind.

Soc.: Shall I, then, let the lot of them flow into the vessel like Homer's very poetical "commingling of mountain glens"?[1]

Pro.: Absolutely.

Soc.: In they go! But now we have to return again to the fountain of pleasure. We cannot any longer carry out our original intention of first mixing only the true parts of each of them together. Our love for every

e kind of knowledge has made us let them all in together, before any of the pleasures.

Pro.: What you say is true.

Soc.: Now it is time for us to decide about pleasures, too, whether we ought to admit the whole tribe in their cases or whether we should at first admit the true ones only.

Pro.: It is much safer if we let the true in first!

Soc.: Let them in, then. But what next? If some turn out to be necessary, should we not mix them in also, as we did in the other case?[2]

Pro.: No reason why not, at least if they really are necessary.

---

1. Cf. *Iliad* 4. 452. The picture in Homer is not nearly as cheerful as Plato's; it is the mixture of the uproar in a fierce battle that is there described.

2. Necessary are the pleasures that are natural restorations of natural lacks, such as hunger and thirst. Although they are accepted into the mixed life as a matter of necessity, they will not appear on the list of goods. If this is not an oversight on Plato's part, it must mean that necessity is not sufficient for goodness.

SOC.: But having decided that it was innocuous or even beneficial to spend 63
our lives in the pursuit of all the arts and crafts, we may now come to the
same conclusion about the pleasures. If it is beneficial and harmless to
live our lives enjoying all the pleasures, then we should mix them all in.
PRO.: So what are we to say in their case, and what are we to do?[1]
SOC.: We should not turn to ourselves with this question, Protarchus, but to
the pleasures themselves, as well as to the different kinds of knowledge, and
find out how they feel about each other by putting the question in this way.[2]
PRO.: What way?   b
SOC.: "My friends, whether you ought to be called 'pleasures' or some
other name,[3] would you prefer to live together with every kind of knowledge or rather to live without it entirely?"—To this I think they cannot
help giving this answer.
PRO.: What answer?
SOC.: What has been said already: "It is neither possible nor beneficial
for one tribe to remain alone, in isolation and unmixed. We would prefer   c
to live side by side with that best kind of knowledge, the kind that understands not only all other things but also each one of us, as far as that is
possible."
PRO.: "An excellent answer," we will reply to them.
SOC.: With justice. But after that we have to raise the question with
intelligence and reason. "Do you have any need for any association with
the pleasures?" That is how we would address reason and knowledge.
"What kinds of pleasures?" they might ask in return.
PRO.: Very likely.
SOC.: Our discussion would then continue as follows: "Will you have any   d
need to associate with the strongest and most intensive pleasures in addition to the true pleasures?" we will ask them. "Why on earth should
we need them, Socrates?" they might reply, "They are a tremendous
impediment to us, since they infect the souls in which they dwell with

---

1. That Protarchus does not gladly welcome them all shows that he has fully accepted
Socrates' reservation and has indeed given up the defense of hedonism.

2. The dialogue within a dialogue is a method Socrates often employed in earlier dialogues.
The plea of the pleasures and the kinds of knowledge recall in particular the plea of the
Laws of Athens in the *Crito* (50c–52a). This also allows Socrates to present the pleasures
themselves as reconciled to a mixed life. So they have deserted Philebus too!

3. Cf. the list of alternative names in the initial statement at 11b.

madness or even prevent our own development altogether. Furthermore,
e they totally destroy most of our offspring, since neglect leads to forgetful-
ness. But as to the true and pure pleasures you mentioned, those regard
as our kin. And besides, also add the pleasures of health and of temperance
and all those that commit themselves to virtue as to their deity and follow
it around everywhere.[1] But to forge an association between reason and
those pleasures that are forever involved with foolishness and other kinds
of vice would be totally unreasonable for anyone who aims at the best and
64 most stable mixture or blend. This is true particularly if he wants to
discover in this mixture what the good is in man and in the universe and
to get some vision of the nature of the good itself."[2] When reason makes
this defense for herself, as well as for memory and right opinion, shall we
not admit that she has spoken reasonably and in accord with her own
standards?

PRO.: Absolutely.

SOC.: But see whether the following is also necessary and without it not
a single thing could come to be?

b PRO.: What is it?

SOC.: Wherever we do not mix in truth nothing could truly come to be
nor remain in existence once it had come to be.[3]

PRO.: How should it?

SOC.: In no way. But now, if there is anything else missing in our mixture,
it is up to you and Philebus to say so. To me at least it seems that our
discussion has arrived at the design of what might be called an incorporeal
order that rules harmoniously over a body possessed by a soul.

PRO.: Count me as one who shares that opinion, Socrates.

---

1. If Plato is consistent in his conception of pleasure as a remedial good, these pleasures
cannot be those of possession but only those of the pursuit of these good states. The phrase
"followers of the god" (*theou opadoi*) recalls the image in the *Phdr.* (252c) of the soul's pursuit
of its kindred deity.

2. This recalls the microcosm-macrocosm argument in 28d–30c. If there is a connection, then we can indeed hope to be able to extrapolate from the good in human life
to the good in the universe and thence to the principle of the good as such.

3. It seems odd that truth should be added as an *extra* ingredient of the mixture,
after pleasure and knowledge. Does the truth of pleasure and knowledge not suffice
for the truth of the whole? Does Plato want to indicate that the mixture not only must
be based on human agreement, but also must have a foundation in reality (a Form
of the mixed life)? The fact that Socrates calls the order of the mixed life the "design
of . . . an incorporeal order . . ." in the next sentence speaks emphatically for such an
interpretation.

V. The solution of the discussion:
the final ranking of goods (64c–67b)

SOC.: Would there be some justification to our claim that we are by now   *c*
standing on the very threshold of the good and of the house[1] of every
member of its family?*

PRO.: It would seem so, to me at least.

SOC.: What ingredient in the mixture ought we to regard as most valuable
and at the same time as the factor that makes it precious to all mankind?
Once we have found it, we will inquire further whether it is more closely
related and akin to pleasure or to reason, in nature as a whole.

PRO.: You are right. This would certainly be very useful in bringing us   *d*
closer to our final verdict.

SOC.: But it is certainly not difficult to see what factor in each mixture it
is that makes it either most valuable or worth nothing at all.

PRO.: What do you mean?

SOC.: There is not a single human being who does not know it.

PRO.: Know what?

SOC.: That any kind of mixture that does not in some way or other possess
measure or the nature of proportion will necessarily corrupt its ingredients
and most of all itself. For there would be no blending in such cases at all   *e*
but really an unconnected medley, the ruin of whatever happens to be
contained in it.[2]

PRO.: Very true.

SOC.: But now we notice that the force of the good has taken refuge in an
alliance with the nature of the beautiful. For measure and proportion
manifest themselves in all areas as beauty and virtue.[3]

PRO.: Undeniably.

SOC.: But we did say that truth is also included along with them in our
mixture?[4]

---

1. For the house, cf. 61b.

2. If the good life is a mixture, it must have the same constituents as the harmonious mixtures
mentioned earlier, i.e. limit and the unlimited (25a–b). So measure and proportion are its
prime condition. That other 'mixtures' are not real mixtures is here confirmed.

3. The principle that beauty is related to measure and proportion is often asserted by Plato;
it was referred to in 51e; 53b.

4. This makes the addition of truth at 64b look rather ad hoc, because Plato likes trinities,
but we have seen that there is a better explanation.

---

* Keeping the reading of the manuscripts with Diès.

PRO.: Indeed.

65 SOC.: Well, then, if we cannot capture the good in *one* form, we will have to take hold of it in a conjunction of three: beauty, proportion, and truth.[1] Let us affirm that these should by right be treated as a unity and be held responsible for what is in the mixture, for its goodness is what makes the mixture itself a good one.

PRO.: Very well stated.

SOC.: Anyone should by now be able to judge between pleasure and
b intelligence, which of the two is more closely related to the supreme good and more valuable among gods and men.

PRO.: Even if it is obvious, it is better to make it explicit in our discussion.

SOC.: So now let us judge each one of the three in relation to pleasure and reason. For we have to see for which of those two we want to grant closer kinship to each of them.

PRO.: You mean to beauty, truth, and measure?

SOC.: Yes. Take up truth first, Protarchus, and, holding it in front of you,
c look at all three: reason, truth, and pleasure. Then, after withholding judgment for a long time, give your answer, whether for you pleasure or reason is more akin to truth.

PRO.: What need is there for any length of time? I think there is an enormous difference. For pleasure is the greatest impostor of all, by general account, and in connection with the pleasures of love, which seem to be the greatest of all, even perjury is pardoned by the gods.[2] Pleasures are perhaps rather like children who don't possess the least bit of reason.
d Reason, by contrast, either is the same as truth or of all things it is most like it and most true.

SOC.: Next look at measure in the same way, and see whether pleasure possesses more of it than intelligence or intelligence more than pleasure.

PRO.: Once again you are setting me a task I am well prepared for. I don't think that one could find anything that is more outside all measure than

1. Why does Plato split up the good into these three concepts? It seems he wants to make clear that he is not giving us a clear and unambiguous definition of the Good. That it "takes refuge" in three concepts means that we can apply these three criteria when we look for goodness. But further Plato does not want to go. Perhaps there is nothing further that can sensibly be said about the Good as such at this juncture, except that it manifests itself in these three ways.

2. It is difficult to say why Protarchus turns to the most intensive form of pleasure in the final arbitration, even though such pleasures have not been accepted in the mixture (cf. Introd. lxv). Protarchus must relate Socrates' question to the genus of pleasure and knowledge as a whole.

pleasure and excessive joy, while nothing more measured than reason and knowledge could ever be found.

SOC.: Well argued. But now go on to the third criterion. Does reason   *e*
contain more beauty than the tribe of pleasures in our estimate, so that reason is more beautiful than pleasure, or is it the other way round?

PRO.: Why, Socrates, no one, awake or dreaming, could ever see intelligence and reason to be ugly; no one could ever have conceived of them as becoming or being ugly, or that they ever will be.

SOC.: Right.

PRO.: In the case of pleasures, by contrast, when we see anyone actively engaged in them, especially those that are most intense, we notice that   *66*
their effect is quite ridiculous, if not outright obscene;[1] we become quite ashamed ourselves and hide them as much as possible from sight, and we confine such activities to the night, as if daylight must not witness such things.

SOC.: So you will announce everywhere, both by sending messengers and saying it in person to those present, that pleasure is not a property of the first rank, nor again of the second, but that first comes what is somehow connected with measure, the measured and the timely, and whatever else is to be considered similar.*[2]

PRO.: That seems at least to be the upshot of our discussion now.

SOC.: The second rank goes to the well-proportioned and beautiful, the   *b*
perfect, the self-sufficient, and whatever else belongs in that family.[3]

PRO.: That seems right.

SOC.: If you give the third rank, as I divine, to reason and intelligence, you cannot stray far from the truth.

PRO.: Perhaps.

SOC.: Nor again if, beside these three, you give fourth place to those things

---

1. Protarchus has obviously internalized Socrates' characterization of the Phileban pleasures at 47a.

2. That measure is the best constituent of the good life is not surprising. Without proper balance there can be no harmonious mixture. So limit in all its applications wins first prize.

3. This class must refer to the harmonious mixtures themselves, the items that have the right measure.

---

* Although the overall sense of the sentence is clear, it ends with a hopelessly corrupt phrase; I have left out the last words in 66b8, since the conjectures offered by Burnet or Diès are no more than guesswork.

c that we defined as the soul's own properties,[1] to the sciences and the arts, and what we called right opinions, since they are more closely related to the good than pleasure at least.

PRO.: Maybe so.

SOC.: The fifth kind will be those pleasures we set apart and defined as painless; we called them the soul's own pure pleasures, since they are attached to the sciences, some of them even to sense-perception.

PRO.: Perhaps.

SOC.: "With the sixth generation the well-ordered song may find its end," says Orpheus. So it seems that our discussion, too, has found its end at

d the determination of the sixth ranking.[2] There remains nothing further to do for us except to give a final touch to what has been said.

PRO.: We have to do that.

SOC.: Come on, then, "the third libation goes to Zeus the Savior," let us call the same argument to witness for the third time.

PRO.: Which one?

SOC.: Philebus declares that every pleasure of any kind is the good. . . .

PRO.: By the "third libation" you appear to mean, as you just stated, that we have to repeat the argument all over from the beginning!

e SOC.: Yes, but let's also hear what follows. In view of all the considerations laid out here and out of distaste for Philebus' position pronounced by countless others on many occasions, I maintained that reason is far superior to pleasure and more beneficial for human life.

PRO.: That is correct.

SOC.: Suspecting that there are many other goods, I said that if something turned out to be better than these two, then I would fight on the side of reason for the second prize against pleasure, so that pleasure would be deprived even of the second rank.

67 PRO.: You did say that.

SOC.: Afterwards it became most sufficiently clear that neither of those two would suffice.

PRO.: Very true.

SOC.: And did it not become clear at this point in our discussion that both

---

1. The separation of reason and intelligence from the lesser sciences has been argued for extensively. That the lesser sciences are here called "the souls' own properties" may signify that they are acquired (as *nous* and *phronesis*, the soul's own faculties, are not).

2. It does not seem that there actually is a sixth rank for the necessary pleasures. For though the text here seems ambiguous, the repetition of the results at 67a14 leaves no doubt that the scale ends with step five.

reason and pleasure had lost any claim that one or the other would be the good itself, since they were lacking in autonomy and in the power of self-sufficiency and perfection?

PRO.: Exactly.

SOC.: Then, when a third competitor showed up, superior to either of them, it became apparent that reason was infinitely more closely related and akin to the character of the victor.

PRO.: Undeniably.

SOC.: And did not pleasure turn out to receive fifth position, according to the verdict we reached in our discussion?

PRO.: Apparently.

SOC.: But not first place, even if all the cattle and horses and the rest of   b
the animals gave testimony by following pleasure.[1] Now, many people accept their testimony, as the seers do that of the birds, and judge that pleasures are most effective in securing the happy life; they even believe that the animal passions are more authoritative witnesses than is the love of argument that is constantly revealed under the guidance of the philosophic muse.

PRO.: We are all agreed now that what you said is as true as possible, Socrates.

SOC.: So will you let me go now?

PRO.: There is still a little missing, Socrates. Surely you will not give up before we do. But I will remind you of what is left![2]

1. Socrates has to 'rub it in': Philebus and his pleasures are relegated to the province of beasts.

2. The dialogue ends but has no real end, just as it had no real beginning. If Protarchus is not just demonstrating his eagerness for more of the philosophic muse, once he has had a taste of it, this may be a reminder that, though the dialogue's main topic, the case of 'pleasure vs. knowledge', is closed, important questions have not been settled (cf. Introd. p. lxvi–vii).